Open up our eyes to see what You see
Open up our minds to dream what You dream
Open up the skies and send revival
Open up our lives
Spirit fall down

We see You're coming
Your glory shines on the earth
We see You're moving
You're fingerprints are here
This is revival

Mark Alan, "This is Revival (Open Up Our Eyes)"
(Emmanuel Christian Center Publishing / BMI © 2014)

Charles Finney's
LECTURES ON REVIVAL

Selected Messages to Ignite You, Your Church and Community

selected and edited for today by
Kevin Senapatiratne
with added study questions

CHRIST CONNECTION
M·E·D·I·A
www.christconnection.cc

Charles Finney's Lectures on Revival: Selected manuscripts to ignite you, your church and community.

Lectures on Revivals of Religion by Charles Finney was first printed in 1835 and revised for publication in 1868. This edition contains selected portions from the 1868 edition, along with additional material, including study questions, action items, and helps for using the material in a congregational or Bible study setting.

Copyright © 2014 Kevin Senapatiratne

ISBN 978-1-312-33178-5

Unless otherwise noted, Scripture quotations are from Scripture taken from the King James Version. Public Domain.

Scripture quotations noted NLT are from The Holy Bible, New Living Translation, copyright 1996. Used by permission of Tyndale House Publishers, Inc., Wheaton, Illinois 60189. All rights reserved.

Table of Contents

Why I Produced this Book   i

Original Prefaces   iii

1. What a revival of religion is   1

2. When a revival is to be expected   19

3. How to promote a revival   37

4. Prevailing Prayer   56

5. The Prayer of Faith   79

6. Meetings for Prayer   103

Afterward   125

Help in Using this Book   126

About this Book   128

Curtain Call   130

Why I Produced this Book

I have been in the church all of my life. I was one of those "born on Saturday and in church on Sunday" kinds of kids. Although to be fair I was born on Saturday and not in church on Sunday, but I have seen a lot of the life of church. I traveled with my parents as a missionary kid when they were raising support to go overseas. It helped me see behind the curtain of what the church is like.

As a teenager I started going to a church that had a youth group which at one point had about 300 kids. We were taught an attitude of believing that what God has done in the past He would do it again. There was a deep hunger for more of God. After high school I stayed on for a year as one of their many leaders while starting Bible College.

It was at some point in this time period that I was first introduced to Charles Finney and his "Lectures on Revival." I was drawn into his practical teaching on how revival comes to the church. Because I was reading that while seeing it worked out in the lives of teenagers his thoughts marked my life.

Now, as I travel and speak at churches on the life of prayer, I often see people with a desire for more of God. They want to experience the New Testament Christianity that they seem to have only read about in the Bible and other books.

Maybe you are one of those people. You long for more of God, but don't even know where to begin. Are the things that God does just happen whenever God "feels in the mood"? When I speak at churches I sometimes have the thought, "Why not in this place?" In the grand scheme of things God could just as easily work in your life and church as any other place in the world. In my study of church history many of the places that God did extraordinary things are the same kind of places that you are at right now.

This book will give you some direction in moving toward the new things that God has for you and your church. When I put this book together I tried to remove the obstacles that might keep you from benefiting from this teaching. The original Lectures on Revival are much longer, but I picked out some of the key ones so you wouldn't be intimidated by the size.

Revival also is not ultimately a solo experience. It should begin to affect the whole community of believers. That is why I added some discussion questions and thoughts for pastors and leaders so that you can experience this as a whole church.

Charles Finney was an evangelist who lived from 1792-1875. He would travel from town to town in the United States and a revival of the church would often happen in that place. When he got older and could not travel any longer he began to pastor one church. It was during this time that *Lectures on Revival* came into existence.

My hope is that as you engage with each lecture your heart would be awakened to believe for all that God has for you, your church and community. My prayer is that this book arrives in your hands at just the right time. Who knows what God will do as you read this? Why not here? Why not now? Why not revival?

The Lecturer's Preface

Let it be remembered, that these Lectures were delivered to my own congregation. They were entered upon, without my having previously marked out any plan or outline of them, and have been pursued, from week to week, as one subject naturally introduced another, and as, from one lecture to another, I saw the state of our people seemed to require.

I consented to have the Editor of the Evangelist report them, upon his own responsibility, because he thought that it might excite a deeper interest in, and extend the usefulness of, his paper. And as I am now a Pastor, and have not sufficient health to labor as an Evangelist, and as it has pleased the Head of the Church to give me some experience in revivals of religion, I thought it possible that, while I was doing the work of a Pastor in my own church, I might, in this way, be of some little service to the churches abroad.

I found a particular inducement to this course, in the fact that on my return from the Mediterranean, I learned, with pain, that the spirit of revival had greatly declined in the United States, and that a spirit of jangling and controversy alarmingly prevailed.

The peculiar circumstances of the church, and the state of revivals, was such, as unavoidably to lead me to the discussion of some points that I would gladly have avoided, had the omission been consistent with my main design, to reach and arouse the church, when she was fast settling down upon her lees.

I am far from setting up the claim of infallibility upon this or any other subject. I have given my own views, so far as I have gone, without pretending to have exhausted the subject, or to have spoken in the best possible manner upon the points I have discussed.

I am too well acquainted with the state of the church, and especially with the state of some of its ministers, to expect to escape without censure. I have felt obliged to say some things that I fear will not, in all instances, be received as kindly as they were intended. But whatever may be the result of saying the truth as it respects some, I have reason to believe, that the great body of praying people will receive and be benefited by what I have said.

What I have said upon the subject of prayer, will not, I am well aware, be understood and received by a certain portion of the church and all I can say is, "He that hath an ear to hear, let him hear."

I had not the most distant idea until recently, that these Lectures, is this, or any other form, would ever grow into a book; but the urgent call for their publication, in a volume, and the fact that I have had repeated assurances that the reading of them in the Evangelist, has been owned and blessed, to the quickening of individuals and churches, and has resulted in the conversion of many sinners, have led me to consent to their publication in this imperfect form.

The Reporter has succeeded, in general, in giving an outline of the Lectures, as they were delivered. His report, however, would, in general, make no more than a full skeleton of what was said on the subject at the time. In justice to the Reporter, I would say, that on reading his reports, in his paper, although there were some

The Lecturer's Preface

mistakes and misapprehensions, yet I have been surprised that, without stenography, he could so nearly report my meaning.

As for literary merit, they have none; nor do they lay claim to any. It was no part of my design to deliver elegant Lectures. They were my most familiar Friday evening discourses; and my great, and I may add my only object, was to have them understood and felt.

In correcting the Lectures for a volume, I have not had time, nor was it thought advisable to remodel them, and change the style in which they had been reported. I have, in some few instances, changed the phraseology, when a thought had been very awkwardly expressed, or when the true idea had not been given. But I have, in nearly every instance, left the sentences as they were reported when the thought was perspicuously expressed, although the style might have been improved by emendation. They were the editor's reports, and as such they must go before the public, with such little additions and alterations, as I have had time to make. Could I have written them out in full, I doubt not but they might have been more acceptable to many readers. But this was impossible, and the only alternative was, to let the public have them as they are, or refuse to let them go out in the form of a volume at all. I am sorry they are not better Lectures, and in a more attracting form; but I have done what I could under the circumstances; and, as it is the wish of many whom I love, and delight to please and honor, to have them, although in this imperfect form, they must have them.

C. G. FINNEY.

Lectures on Revival of Religion

By perusing the above Preface, the reader will get a clue to the time and circumstances that led to the delivery and publication of these Lectures. In revising them for a new edition, I have done little more than correct the phraseology in a few instances, add a few foot-notes, and replace the last two Lectures by newly-written ones on the same texts, and prepared especially for this edition. These Lectures are distinct from the course I deliver to my theological class upon the same subject. That course I may publish before my death. These Lectures have been translated in the Welsh and French languages, and have been very extensively circulated wherever the English or either of those languages is understood. One house in London published 80,000 copies In English. They are still in type and in market in Europe, and I have the great satisfaction of knowing that they have been made a great blessing to thousands of souls. Consequently, I have not thought it wise to recast them for the sake of giving them a more attractive form. God has owned and blessed the reading of them as they have been, and with the exceptions above noticed, I have given them to the present and coming generations. If the reader will peruse and remember the foregoing preface, he will understand what I said of the church and some of the ministers, and why I said it. I beseech my brethren not to take amiss what I have said, but rather to be assured that every sentence has been spoken in love, and often with a sorrowful heart. May God continue to add His blessing to the reading of these Lectures.

THE AUTHOR.
OBERLIN COLLEGE, Oct. 22, 1868.

Advertisement by the Reporter

The work of reporting these Lectures was undertaken for the purpose of increasing the interest and usefulness of the New York Evangelist. The Reporter is wholly unacquainted with short-hand, and has, therefore, only aimed to give a sketch of the leading thoughts of the discourse. It is hardly necessary to mention that Mr. Finney never writes his sermons, but guides his course of argument by a skeleton, or brief, carefully prepared, and so compact, that it can be written on one side of a card, about half as large as one of these printed pages. His manner is direct, and his language colloquial and Saxon, and his illustrations are drawn from the commonest incidents and maxims of life. The Reporter has aimed to preserve, as much as he could, the style of the speaker, and is thought to have been in some degree successful. If, in any cases, by letting his language run in a colloquial strain, he has made the copy more simple and homely than the original, he hopes to be pardoned easily for a fault by no means prevalent.

If anyone should attempt to criticize the style of these Reports, he will assuredly lose his labor; for the only ambition of the Reporter has been, to make such a use of language as should fully convey the meaning, and fairly exhibit the manner, of the Lecturer. When words have done this, they have done their great work. The notes were taken with a pencil, and transcribed in great haste, and sent to the printer without revision. In preparing them for publication, in this form, Mr. Finney has reviewed them with reference only to this point – the correct expression of the sentiment. The style of an off-hand sketch has been preserved, partly of choice, and partly from necessity. There was no time to remodel the work, and the public voice seemed to be, that it was more attractive and more useful in its present condensed form. Mr. Finney has, therefore, done little more than to amend where the Reporter misapprehended the meaning, or did not express it with sufficient distinctness. He has enlarged in a few places where the illustrations, as given by the Reporter, seemed to be incomplete.

My labor with these sketches is now done; and its results are sent forth in this permanent form, with the prayer, that God would employ the book, as he has already done the newspaper edition, to rouse, and teach, and strengthen his people, and to guide, unite, and encourage zealous Christians of all classes, in the great duty of saving sinners.

J.L.

chapter one
What a Revival of Religion is

> *O Lord, revive thy work in the midst of the years,*
> *in the midst of the years make known;*
> *in wrath remember mercy.*
>
> HABAKKUK 3:2

It is supposed that the prophet Habakkuk was contemporary with Jeremiah, and that this prophecy was uttered in anticipation of the Babylonish captivity. Looking at the judgments which were speedily to come upon his nation, the soul of the prophet was wrought up to an agony, and he cries out in his distress, "O Lord, revive thy work." As if he had said, "O Lord, grant that thy judgments may not make Israel desolate. In the midst of these awful years, let the judgments of God be made the means of reviving religion among us. In wrath remember mercy."

Religion is the work of man. It is something for man to do. It consists in obeying God with and from the heart. It is man's duty. It is true, God induces him to do it. He influences him by his Spirit, because of his great wickedness and reluctance to obey. If it were not necessary for God to influence men – if men were disposed to obey God, there would be no occasion to pray, "O Lord, revive thy work." The ground of necessity for such a prayer is, that men are wholly indisposed to obey; and unless God interpose the influence of his Spirit, not a man on earth will ever obey the commands of God.

A "Revival of Religion" presupposes a declension. Almost all the religion in the world has been produced by revivals. God has found it necessary to take advantage of the excitability there is in mankind, to produce powerful excitements among them, before he can lead them to obey. Men are so spiritually sluggish, there are so many things to lead their minds off from religion, and to oppose the influence of the Gospel, that it is necessary to raise an excitement among them, till the tide rises so high as to sweep away the opposing obstacles. They must be so excited that they will break over these counteracting influences, before they will obey God. Not that excited feeling is religion, for it is not; but it is excited desire, appetite and feeling that prevents religion. The will is, in a sense, enslaved by the carnal and worldly desires. Hence it is necessary to awaken men to a sense of guilt and danger, and thus produce an excitement of counter feeling and desire which will break the power of carnal and worldly desire and leave the will free to obey God.

Look back at the history of the Jews, and you will see that God used to maintain religion among them by special occasions, when there would be a great excitement, and people would turn to the Lord. And after they had been thus revived, it would be but a short time before there would be so many counteracting influences brought to bear upon them, that religion would decline, and keep on declining, till God could have time – so to speak – to convict them of sin by his Spirit and rebuke them by his providence, and thus so gain the attention of the masses to the great subject of salvation, as to produce a widespread awakening of religious interest, and consequently a revival of religion. Then the counteracting causes would again operate, and religion would decline, and the nation would be swept away in the vortex of luxury, idolatry, and pride.

There is so little principle in the church, so little firmness and stability of purpose, that unless the religious feelings are awakened and kept excited, counter worldly feeling and excitement will prevail, and men will not obey God. They have so little knowledge, and their principles are so weak, that unless they are excited, they will go back from the path of duty, and do nothing to promote the glory of God. The state of the world is still such, and probably will be till the millennium is fully come, that religion must be mainly promoted by means of revivals. How long and how often has the experiment been tried, to bring the church to act steadily for God, without these periodical excitements? Many good men have supposed, and still suppose, that the best way to promote religion, is to go along uniformly, and gather in the ungodly gradually, and without excitement. But however sound such reasoning may appear in the abstract, facts demonstrate its futility. If the church were far enough advanced in knowledge, and had stability of principle enough to keep awake, such a course would do; but the church is so little enlightened, and there are so many counteracting causes, that she will not go steadily to work without a special interest being awakened. As the millennium advances, it is probable that these periodical excitements will be unknown. Then the church will be enlightened, and the counteracting causes removed, and the entire church will be in a state of habitual and steady obedience to God. The entire church will stand and take the infant mind, and cultivate it for God.

Children will be trained up in the way they should go, and there will be no such torrents of worldliness, and fashion, and covetousness, to bear away the piety of the church, as soon as the excitement of a revival is withdrawn.

It is very desirable it should be so. It is very desirable that the church should go on steadily in a course of obedience without these excitements. Such excitements are liable to injure the health. Our nervous system is so strung that any powerful excitement, if long continued, injures our health and unfits us for duty. If religion is ever to have a pervading influence in the world, it cannot be so; this spasmodic religion must be done away. Then it will be uncalled for. Christians will not sleep the greater part of the time, and once in a while wake up, and rub their eyes, and bluster about, and vociferate a little while, and then go to sleep again. Then there will be no need that ministers should wear themselves out, and kill themselves, by their efforts to roll back the flood of worldly influence that sets in upon the church. But as yet the state of the Christian world is such, that to expect to promote religion without excitements is unphilosophical and absurd. The great political, and other worldly excitements that agitate Christendom, are all unfriendly to religion, and divert the mind from the interests of the soul. Now these excitements can only be counteracted by religious excitements. And until there is religious principle in the world to put down irreligious excitements, it is vain to try to promote religion, except by counteracting excitements. This is true in philosophy, and it is a historical fact.

It is altogether improbable that religion will ever make progress among heathen nations except through the influence of revivals. The attempt is now making to do it by education, and other cautious and gradual improvements. But so long as the laws of mind remain what they are, it cannot be done in this way. There must be excitement sufficient to wake up the dormant moral powers, and roll back the tide of degradation and sin. And precisely so far as our own land approximates to heathenism, it is impossible for God or man to promote religion in such a state of things but by powerful excitements. This is evident from the fact that this has always been the way in which God has done it. God does not create these excitements, and choose this method to promote religion for nothing or without reason. Where mankind are so reluctant to obey God, they will not act until they are excited. For instance, how many there are who know that they ought to be religious, but they are afraid if they become pious they shall be laughed at by their companions. Many are wedded to idols, others are procrastinating repentance, until they are settled in life, or until they have secured some favorite worldly interest. Such persons never will give up their false shame, or relinquish their ambitious schemes, till they are so excited by a sense of guilt and danger that they cannot contain themselves any longer.

These remarks are designed only as an introduction to the discourse. I shall now proceed with the main design, to show what a revival of religion is not, what it is, and the agencies employed in promoting it.

Revival is not a Miracle

Revivals were formerly regarded as miracles. And it has been so by some even in our day. And others have ideas on the subject so loose and unsatisfactory, that if they would only think, they would see their absurdity. For a long time, it was supposed by the church, that a revival was a miracle, an interposition of Divine power which they had nothing to do with, and which they had no more agency in producing, than they had in producing thunder, or a storm of hail, or an earthquake. It is only within a few years that ministers generally have supposed revivals were to be promoted, by the use of means designed and adapted specially to that object. Even in New England, it has been supposed that revivals came just as showers do, sometimes in one town, and sometimes in another, and that ministers and churches could do nothing more to produce them than they could to make showers of rain come on their own town, when they are falling on a neighboring town.

It used to be supposed that a revival would come about once in fifteen years, and all would be converted that God intended to save, and then they must wait until another crop came forward on the stage of life. Finally, the time got shortened down to five years, and they supposed there might be a revival about as often as that.

I have heard a fact in relation to one of these pastors, who supposed revivals might come about once in five years. There had been a revival in his congregation. The next year, there was a revival in a neighboring town, and he went there to preach, and staid several days, till he got his soul all engaged in the work. He returned home on Saturday, and went into his study to prepare for the Sabbath. And his soul was in an agony. He thought how many adult persons there were in his congregation at enmity with God – so many still unconverted, so many persons die yearly, such a portion of them unconverted – if a revival does not come under five years, so many adult heads of families will be in hell. He put down his calculations on paper, and embodied them in his sermon for the next day, with his heart bleeding at the dreadful picture. As I understood it, he did not do this with any expectation of a revival, but he felt deeply, and poured out his heart to his people.

And that sermon awakened forty heads of families, and a powerful revival followed; and so his theory about a revival once in five years was all exploded. Thus God has overthrown, generally, the theory that revivals are miracles.

***

A miracle has been generally defined to be, a Divine interference, setting aside or suspending the laws of nature. It is not a miracle in this sense. *All the laws of matter and mind remain in force.* They are neither suspended nor set aside in a revival.

It is not a miracle according to another definition of the term miracle – something above the powers of nature. *There is nothing in religion beyond the ordinary powers of nature.* It consists entirely in the right exercise of the powers of nature. It is just that, and nothing else. When mankind become religious, they are not enabled to put forth exertions which they were unable before to put forth. They only exert the powers they had before in a different way, and use them for the glory of God.

It is not a miracle, or dependent on a miracle, in any sense. It is a purely philosophical result of the right use of the constituted means – as much so as any other effect produced by the application of means. There may be a miracle among its antecedent causes, or there may not. The apostles employed miracles, simply as a means by which they arrested attention to their message, and established its divine authority. But the miracle was not the revival. The miracle was one thing; the revival that followed it was quite another thing. The revivals in the apostles' days were connected with miracles, but they were not miracles.

I said that a revival is the result of the right use of the appropriate means. The means which God has enjoined for the production of a revival, doubtless have a natural tendency to produce a revival. Otherwise God would not have enjoined them. But means will not produce a revival, we all know, without the blessing of God. No more will grain. When it is sowed, produce a crop without the blessing of God. It is impossible for us to say that there is not as direct an influence or agency from God, to produce a crop of grain, as there is to produce a revival. What are the laws of nature according to which it is supposed that grain yields a crop? They are nothing but the constituted manner of the operations of God. In the Bible, the word of God is compared to grain, and preaching is compared to sowing seed, and the results to the springing up and growth of the crop. And the result is just as philosophical in the one case, as in the other, and is as naturally connected with the cause; or, more correctly, a revival is as naturally a result of the use of the appropriate means as a crop is of the use of its appropriate means. It is true that religion does not properly belong to the category of cause and effect; but although it is not caused by means, yet it has its occasion, and may as naturally and certainly result from its occasion as a crop does from its cause.

I wish this idea to be impressed on all your minds, for there has long been an idea prevalent that promoting religion has something very peculiar in it, not to be judged of by the ordinary rules of cause and effect; in short, that there is no connection of the means with the result, and no tendency in the means to produce the effect. No doctrine is more dangerous than this to the prosperity of the church, and nothing more absurd.

Suppose a man were to go and preach this doctrine among farmers, about their sowing grain. Let him tell them that God is a sovereign, and will give them a crop only when it pleases him, and that for them to plow and plant and labor as if they expected to raise a crop is very wrong, and taking the work out of the hands of God, that it interferes with his sovereignty, and is going on in their own strength: and that there is no connection between the means and the result on which they can depend. And now, suppose the farmers should believe such doctrine. Why, they would starve the world to death.

Just such results will follow from the church's being persuaded that promoting religion is somehow so mysteriously a subject of Divine sovereignty, that there is no natural connection between the means and the end. What are the results? Why, generation after generation has gone down to hell. No doubt more than five thousand millions have gone down to hell, while the church has been dreaming, and waiting for God to save them without the use of means. It has been the devil's most successful means of destroying souls. The connection is as clear in religion as it is when the farmer sows his grain.

There is one fact under the government of God, worthy of universal notice, and of everlasting remembrance; which is, that the most useful and important things are most easily and certainly obtained by the use of the appropriate means. This is evidently a principle in the Divine administration. Hence, all the necessaries of life are obtained with great certainty by the use of the simplest means. The luxuries are more difficult to obtain; the means to procure them are more intricate and less certain in their results; while things absolutely hurtful and poisonous, such as alcohol and the like, are often obtained only by torturing nature, and making use of a kind of infernal sorcery to procure the death-dealing abomination. This principle holds true in moral government, and as spiritual blessings are of surpassing importance, we should expect their attainment to be connected with great certainty with the use of the appropriate means; and such we find to be the fact;

and I fully believe that could facts be known, it would be found that when the appointed means have been rightly used, spiritual blessings have been obtained with greater uniformity than temporal ones.

What a Revival is

It is the renewal of the first love of Christians, resulting in the awakening and conversion of sinners to God. In the popular sense, a revival of religion in a community is the arousing, quickening, and reclaiming of the more or less backslidden church and the more or less general awakening of all classes, and insuring attention to the claims of God.

It presupposes that the church is sunk down in a backslidden state, and a revival consists in the return of a church from her backslidings, and in the conversion of sinners.

A revival always includes conviction of sin on the part of the church. Backslidden professors cannot wake up and begin right away in the service of God, without deep searchings of heart. The fountains of sin need to be broken up. In a true revival, Christians are always brought under such convictions; they see their sins in such a light, that often they find it impossible to maintain a hope of their acceptance with God. It does not always go to that extent; but there are always, in a genuine revival, deep convictions of sin, and often cases of abandoning all hope.

Backslidden Christians will be brought to repentance. A revival is nothing else than a new beginning of obedience to God. Just as in the case of a converted sinner, the first step is a deep repentance, a breaking down of heart, a getting down into the dust before God, with deep humility, and forsaking of sin.

What a Revival of Religion Is

Christians will have their faith renewed. While they are in their backslidden state they are blind to the state of sinners. Their hearts are as hard as marble. The truths of the Bible only appear like a dream. They admit it to be all true; their conscience and their judgment assent to it; but their faith does not see it standing out in bold relief, in all the burning realities of eternity. But when they enter into a revival, they no longer see men as trees walking, but they see things in that strong light which will renew the love of God in their hearts. This will lead them to labor zealously to bring others to him. They will feel grieved that others do not love God, when they love him so much. And they will set themselves feelingly to persuade their neighbors to give him their hearts. So their love to men will be renewed. They will be filled with a tender and burning love for souls. They will have a longing desire for the salvation of the whole world. They will be in an agony for individuals whom they want to have saved – their friends, relations, enemies. They will not only be urging them to give their hearts to God, but they will carry them to God in the arms of faith, and with strong crying and tears beseech God to have mercy on them, and save their souls from endless burnings.

A revival breaks the power of the world and of sin over Christians. It brings them to such vantage ground that they get a fresh impulse towards heaven. They have a new foretaste of heaven, and new desires after union with God; and the charm of the world is broken, and the power of sin overcome.

When the churches are thus awakened and reformed, *the reformation and salvation of sinners will follow*, going through the same stages of conviction, repentance, and reformation. Their hearts will be broken down and changed. Very often the most abandoned profligates are among the subjects. Harlots, and drunkards, and infidels, and all sorts of abandoned characters, are awakened and converted. The worst among human beings are softened, and reclaimed, and made to appear as lovely specimens of the beauty of holiness.

The Agencies that Carry Revival Forward

Many people have supposed God's sovereignty to be something very different from what it is. They have supposed it to be such an arbitrary disposal of events, and particularly of the gift of his Spirit, as precluded a rational employment of means for promoting a revival of religion. But there is no evidence from the Bible that God exercises any such sovereignty as that. There are no facts to prove it. But everything goes to show that God has connected means with the end through all the departments of his government—in nature and in grace. There is no natural event in which his own agency is not concerned. He has not built the creation like a vast machine that will go on alone without his further care. He has not retired from the universe, to let it work for itself. This is mere atheism. He exercises a universal superintendence and control. And yet every event in nature has been brought about by means. He neither administers providence nor grace with that sort of sovereignty that dispenses with the use of means. There is no more sovereignty in one than in the other.

And yet some people are terribly alarmed at all direct efforts to promote a revival, and they cry out, "You are trying to get up a revival in your own strength. Take care; you are interfering with the sovereignty of God. Better keep along in the usual course, and let God give a revival when he thinks it is best. God is a sovereign, and it is very wrong for you to attempt to get up a revival, just because you think a revival is needed." This is just such preaching as the devil wants. And men cannot do the devil's work more effectually than by preaching up the sovereignty of God, as a reason why we should not put forth efforts to produce a revival.

**

Ordinarily, there are three agents employed in the work of conversion, and one instrument. The agents are God, some person who brings the truth to bear on the mind, and the sinner himself. The instrument is the truth. There are always two agents, God and the sinner, employed and active in every case of genuine conversion.

The agency of God is two-fold; by his Providence and by his Spirit. By his providential government, he so arranges events as to bring the sinner's mind and the truth in contact. He brings the sinner where the truth reaches his ears or his eyes. It is often interesting to trace the manner in which God arranges events so as to bring this about, and how he sometimes makes everything seem to favor a revival. The state of the weather, and of the public health, and other circumstances concur to make everything just right to favor the application of truth with the greatest possible efficacy. How he sometimes sends a minister along, just at the time he is wanted! How he brings out a particular truth, just at the particular time when the individual it is fitted to reach is in the way to hear!

God's special agency by his Holy Spirit. Having direct access to the mind, and knowing infinitely well the whole history and state of each individual sinner, he employs that truth which is best adapted to his particular case, and then sets it home with Divine power. He gives it such vividness, strength, and power, that the sinner quails, and throws down his weapons of rebellion, and turns to the Lord. Under his influence, the truth burns and cuts its way like fire. He makes the truth stand out in such aspects, that it crushes the proudest man down with the weight of a mountain. If men were disposed to obey God, the truth is given with sufficient clearness in the Bible; and from preaching they could learn all that is necessary for them to know. But because they are wholly disinclined to obey it, God clears it up before their minds, and pours in a blaze of convincing light upon their souls, which they cannot withstand, and they yield to it, and obey God, and are saved.

The agency of men is commonly employed. Men are not mere instruments in the hands of God. Truth is the instrument. The preacher is a moral agent in the work; he acts; he is not a mere passive instrument; he is voluntary in promoting the conversion of sinners.

The agency of the sinner himself. The conversion of a sinner consists in his obeying the truth. It is therefore impossible it should take place without his agency, for it consists in his acting right. He is influenced to this by the agency of God, and by the agency of men. Men act on their fellow-men, not only by language, but by their looks, their tears, and their daily deportment. See that impenitent man there, who has a pious wife. Her very looks, her tenderness, her solemn, compassionate dignity, softened and moulded into the image of Christ are a sermon to him all the time. He has to turn his mind away, because it is such a reproach to him. He feels a sermon ringing in his ears all day long.

Mankind is accustomed to read the countenances of their neighbors. Sinners often read the state of a Christian's mind in his eyes. If his eyes are full of levity, or worldly anxiety and contrivance, sinners read it. If they are full of the Spirit of God, sinners read it; and they are often led to conviction by barely seeing the countenance of Christians.

An individual once went into a manufactory to see the machinery. His mind was solemn, as he had been where there was a revival. The people who labored there all knew him by sight, and knew who he was. A young lady who was at work saw him, and whispered some foolish remark to her companion, and laughed. The person stopped and looked at her with a feeling of grief. She stopped, her thread broke, and she was so much agitated she could not join it. She looked out at the window to compose herself, and then tried again; again and again she strove to recover her self-command. At length she sat down, overcome with her feelings. The person then approached and spoke with her; she soon manifested a deep sense of sin. The feeling spread through the establishment like fire, and in a few hours almost every person employed there was under conviction, so much so, that the owner, though a worldly man, was astounded, and requested to have the works stop and have a prayer meeting; for he said it was a great deal more important to have these people converted than to have the works go on. And in a few days, the owner and nearly every person employed in the establishment were hopefully converted. The eye of this individual, his solemn countenance, his compassionate feeling, rebuked the levity of the young woman, and brought her under conviction of sin: and this whole revival followed, probably in a great measure, from so small an incident.

If Christians have deep feeling on the subject of religion themselves, they will produce deep feeling wherever they go. And if they are cold, or light and trifling, they inevitably destroy all deep feeling, even in awakened sinners.

I knew a case, once, of an individual who was very anxious, but one day I was grieved to find that her convictions seemed to be all gone. I asked her what she had been doing. She told me she had been spending the afternoon at such a place, among some professors of religion, not thinking that it would dissipate her convictions to spend an afternoon with professors of religion. But they were trifling and vain, and thus her convictions were lost. And no doubt those professors of religion, by their folly, destroyed a soul, for her convictions did not return.

The church is required to use the means for the conversion of sinners. Sinners cannot properly be said to use the means for their own conversion. The church uses the means. What sinners do is to submit to the truth, or to resist it. It is a mistake of sinners, to think they are using means for their own conversion. The whole drift of a revival, and everything about it, is designed to present the truth to your mind, for your obedience or resistance.

The Necessity of Revival

You see the error of those who are beginning to think that religion can be better promoted in the world without revivals, and who are disposed to give up all efforts to produce religious awakenings. Because there are evils arising in some instances out of great excitements on the subject of religion, they are of opinion that it is best to dispense with them altogether. This cannot, and must not be. True, there is danger of abuses. In cases of great religious as well as all other excitements, more or less incidental evils may be expected of course. But this is no reason why they should be given up. The best things are always liable to abuses. Great and manifold evils have originated in the providential and moral governments of God. But these foreseen perversions and evils were not considered a sufficient reason for giving them up.

What a Revival of Religion Is

For the establishment of these governments was on the whole the best that could be done for the production of the greatest amount of happiness. So in revivals of religion, it is found by experience, that in the present state of the world, religion cannot be promoted to any considerable extent without them. The evils which are sometimes complained of, when they are real, are incidental, and of small importance when compared with the amount of good produced by revivals. The sentiment should not be admitted by the church for a moment, that revivals may be given up. It is fraught with all that is dangerous to the interests of Zion, is death to the cause of missions, and brings in its train the damnation of the world.

***

Finally, I have a proposal to make to you who are here present. I have not commenced this course of Lectures on Revivals to get up a curious theory of my own on the subject. I would not spend my time and strength merely to give you instructions, to gratify your curiosity, and furnish you something to talk about. I have no idea of preaching about revivals. It is not my design to preach so as to have you able to say at the close, "We understand all about revivals now," while you do nothing. But I wish to ask you a question. What do you hear lectures on revivals for? Do you mean that whenever you are convinced what your duty is in promoting a revival, you will go to work and practise it?

Will you follow the instructions I shall give you from the word of God, and put them in practise in your own lives? Will you bring them to bear upon your families, your acquaintance, neighbors, and through the city? Or will you spend the winter in learning about revivals, and do nothing for them? I want you, as fast as you learn anything on the subject of revivals, to put it in practice, and go to work and see if you cannot promote a revival among sinners here. If you will not do this, I wish you to let me know at the beginning, so that I need not waste my strength. You ought to decide now whether you will do this or not. You know that we call sinners to decide on the spot whether they will obey the Gospel. And we have no more authority to let you take time to deliberate whether you will obey God, than we have to let sinners do so. We call on you to unite now in a solemn pledge to God, that you will do your duty as fast as you learn what it is, and to pray that He will pour out his Spirit upon this church and upon all the city this winter.

Questions:

1. What comes to mind when you hear the word "revival"?

2. How does this chapter challenge your current view of revival?

3. What has been your experience with anything like the revival he describes?

Action:

Take some time to pray about revival for you, your group and church.

chapter two
When a Revival is to be Expected

*Won't you revive us again,
so your people can rejoice in you?*

Psalm 85:6 NLT

    This Psalm seems to have been written soon after the return of the people of Israel from the Babylonish captivity; as you will easily see from the language at the commencement of it. The Psalmist felt that God had been very favorable to the people, and while contemplating the goodness of the Lord in bringing them back from the land where they had been carried away captive, and while looking at the prospects before them, he breaks out into a prayer for a Revival of Religion. "Won't you revive us again, so your people can rejoice in you?" Since God in his providence had re-established the ordinances of his house among them, he prays that there may be also a revival of religion, to crown the work.
    Last Friday evening I attempted to show what a Revival of Religion is not; what a Revival is; and the agencies to be employed

in promoting it. The topics to which I wish to call your attention tonight are when a revival of religion is needed, the importance of a Revival when it is needed, and when a revival of religion may be expected.

When is a Revival of Religion Needed?

When *there is a want of brotherly love* and Christian confidence among professors of religion, then a revival is needed. Then there is a loud call for God to revive his work. When Christians have sunk down into a low and backslidden state, they neither have, nor ought to have, nor is there reason to have, the same love and confidence toward each other, as when they are all alive, and active, and living holy lives. The love of benevolence may be the same, but not the love of complacency. God loves all men with the love of benevolence, but he does not feel the love of complacency toward any but those who live holy. Christians do not and cannot love each other with the love of complacency, only in proportion to their holiness. If Christian love is the love of the image of Christ in his people, then it never can be exercised only where that image really or apparently exists. A person must reflect the image of Christ, and show the spirit of Christ, before other Christians can love him with the love of complacency. It is in vain to call on Christians to love one another with the love of complacency, as Christians, when they are sunk down in stupidity. They see nothing in each other to produce this love. It is next to impossible that they should feel otherwise toward each other, than they do toward sinners. Merely knowing that they belong to the church, or seeing them occasionally at the communion table, will not produce Christian love, unless they see the image of Christ.

When a Revival is to be Expected

When there are dissensions, and jealousies, and evil speakings among professors of religion, then there is great need of a revival. These things show that Christians have got far from God, and it is time to think earnestly of a revival. Religion cannot prosper with such things in the church, and nothing can put an end to them like a revival.

When there is a worldly spirit in the church. It is manifest that the church is sunk down into a low and backslidden state, when you see Christians conform to the world in dress, equipage, parties, seeking worldly amusements, reading novels, and other books such as the world read. It shows that they are far from God, and that there is great need of a Revival of Religion.

When the church finds its members falling into gross and scandalous sins, then it is time for the church to awake and cry to God for a Revival of Religion. When such things are taking place, as give the enemies of religion an occasion for reproach, it is time for the church to ask God, "What will become of thy great name?"

When there is a spirit of controversy in the church or in the land, a revival is needful. The spirit of religion is not the spirit of controversy. There can be no prosperity in religion, where the spirit of controversy prevails.

When the wicked triumph over the church, and revile them, it is time to seek for a Revival of Religion.

When sinners are careless and stupid, and sinking into hell unconcerned, it is time the church should bestir themselves. It is as much the duty of the church to awake, as it is of the firemen to awake when a fire breaks out in the night in a great city. The church ought to put out the fires of hell which are laying hold of the wicked. Sleep! Should the firemen sleep, and let the whole city burn down: what would be thought of such firemen? And yet their guilt would not compare with the guilt of Christians who sleep while sinners around them are sinking stupid into the fires of hell.

The Importance of a Revival in Such Circumstances

A Revival of Religion is *the only possible thing that can wipe away the reproach which covers the church, and restore religion to the place it ought to have in the estimation of the public*. Without a revival, this reproach will cover the church more and more, until it is overwhelmed with universal contempt. You may do anything else you please, and you can change the aspects of society in some respects, but you will do no real good; you only make it worse without a Revival of Religion. You may go and build a splendid new house of worship, and line your seats with damask, put up a costly pulpit, and get a magnificent organ, and everything of that kind, to make a show and dash, and in that way you may procure a sort of respect for religion among the wicked, but it does no good in reality. It rather does hurt. It misleads them as to the real nature of religion; and so far from converting them, it carries them farther away from salvation. Look wherever they have surrounded the altar of Christianity with splendor, and you will find that the impression produced is contrary to the true nature of religion. There must be a waking up of energy, on the part of Christians, and an outpouring of God's Spirit, or the world will laugh at the church.

Nothing else will restore Christian love and confidence among church members. Nothing but a Revival of Religion can restore it, and nothing else ought to restore it. There is no other way to wake up that love of Christians for one another, which is sometimes felt, when they have such love as they cannot express. You cannot have

When a Revival is to be Expected

such love without confidence; and you cannot restore confidence without such evidence of piety as is seen in a revival. If a minister finds he has lost in any degree the confidence of his people, he ought to labor for a revival as the only means of regaining their confidence. I do not mean that this should be his motive in laboring for a revival, to regain the confidence of his people, but that a revival through his instrumentality, and ordinarily nothing else, will restore to him the confidence of the praying part of his people. So if an elder or private member of the church finds his brethren cold towards him, there is but one way to remedy it. It is by being revived himself, and pouring out from his eyes and from his life the splendor of the image of Christ. This spirit will catch and spread in the church, and confidence will be renewed, and brotherly love prevail again.

At such a time a Revival of Religion is indispensable *to avert the judgments of God from the church*. This would be strange preaching, if revivals are only miracles, and if the church has no more agency in producing them, than it has in making a thunder storm. To say to the church, that unless there is a revival you may expect judgments, would then be as ridiculous as to say, If you do not have a thunder storm, you may expect judgments. The fact is, that Christians are more to blame for not being revived, than sinners are for not being converted. And if they are not awakened, they may know assuredly that God will visit them with his judgments. How often God visited the Jewish church with judgments, because they would not repent and be revived at the call of his prophets! How often have we seen churches, and even whole denominations, cursed with a curse, because they would not wake up and seek the Lord, and pray, "Won't you revive us again, so your people can rejoice in you?"

Nothing but a Revival of Religion can *preserve such a church from annihilation*. A church declining in this way cannot continue to exist without a revival. If it receives new members, they will, for the most part, be made up of ungodly persons. Without revivals there will not ordinarily be as many persons converted as will die off in a year. There have been churches in this country where the members have died off, and there were no revivals to convert others in their place, till the church has run out, and the organization has been dissolved.

Nothing but a Revival of Religion can *prevent the means of grace from doing a great injury to the ungodly*. Without a revival, they will grow harder and harder under preaching, and will experience a more horrible damnation than they would if they had never heard the Gospel. Your children and your friends will go down to a much more horrible fate in hell, in consequence of the means of grace, if there are no revivals to convert them to God. Better were it for them if there were no means of grace, no sanctuary, no Bible, no preaching, and if they had never heard the Gospel, than to live and die where there is no revival. The Gospel is the savor of death unto death, if it is not made a savor of life unto life.

There is *no other way in which a church can be sanctified, grow in grace, and be fitted for heaven*. What is growing in grace? Is it hearing sermons and getting some new notions about religion? No – no such thing. The Christian who does this, and nothing more, is getting worse and worse, more and more hardened, and every week it is more difficult to rouse him up to duty.

* * *

When a Revival May Be Expected

When the providence of God indicates that a revival is at hand. The indications of God's providence are sometimes so plain as to amount to a revelation of his will. There is a conspiring of events to open the way, a preparation of circumstances to favor a revival, so that those who are looking out can see that a revival is at hand, just as plainly as if it had been revealed from Heaven. Cases have occurred in this country, where the providential manifestations were so plain, that those who are careful observers, felt no hesitation in saying that God was coming to pour out his Spirit, and grant a revival of religion. There are various ways for God to indicate his will to a people--sometimes by giving them peculiar means, sometimes by peculiar and alarming events, sometimes by remarkably favoring the employment of means, by the weather, health, etc.

When the wickedness of the wicked grieves and humbles and distresses Christians. Sometimes Christians do not seem to mind anything about the wickedness around them. Or if they talk about it, it is in a cold, and callous, and unfeeling way, as if they despaired of a reformation: they are disposed to scold at sinners – not to feel the compassion of the Son of God for them. But sometimes the conduct of the wicked drives Christians to prayer, and breaks them down, and makes them sorrowful and tender-hearted, so that they can weep day and night, and instead of scolding and reproaching them, they pray earnestly for them. Then you may expect a revival. Indeed this is a revival begun already. Sometimes the wicked will get up an opposition to religion. And when this drives Christians to their knees in prayer to God, with strong crying and tears, you may be certain there is going to be a revival. The prevalence of wickedness is no evidence at all that there is not going to be a revival. That is often God's time to work. When the enemy cometh in like a flood, the Spirit of the Lord lifts up a standard against him. Often the first indication of a revival, is the devil's getting up something new in opposition. It will invariably have one of two effects. It will either drive Christians to God, or it will drive them farther away from God, to some carnal policy or other that will only make things worse. Frequently the most outrageous wickedness of the ungodly is followed by a revival. If Christians are made to feel that they have no hope but in God, and if they have sufficient feeling left to care for the honor of God and the salvation of the souls of the impenitent, there will certainly be a revival. Let hell boil over if it will, and spew out as many devils as there are stones in the pavements, if it only drives Christians to God in prayer--they cannot hinder a revival. Let Satan get up a row, and sound his horn as loud as he pleases; if Christians will only be humbled and pray, they shall soon see God's naked arm in a revival of religion. I have known instances where a revival has broken in upon the ranks of the enemy, almost as suddenly as a clap of thunder, and scattered them – taken the very ringleaders as trophies, and broken up their party in an instant.

A revival may be expected *when Christians have a spirit of prayer for a revival*. That is, when they pray as if their hearts were set upon a revival. Sometimes Christians are not engaged in prayer for a revival, not even when they are warm in prayer. Their minds are upon something else; they are praying for something else – the salvation of the heathen and the like – and not for a revival among themselves. But when they feel the want of a revival, they pray for it; they feel for their own families and neighborhoods, and pray

When a Revival is to be Expected

for them as if they could not be denied. What constitutes a spirit of prayer? Is it many prayers and warm words? No. Prayer is the state of the heart. The spirit of prayer is a state of continual desire and anxiety of mind for the salvation of sinners. It is something that weighs them down. It is the same, so far as the philosophy of the mind is concerned, as when a man is anxious for some worldly interest. A Christian who has this spirit of prayer feels anxious for souls. It is the subject of his thoughts all the time, and makes him look and act as if he had a load on his mind. He thinks of it by day, and dreams of it by night. This is properly praying without ceasing. The man's prayers seem to flow from his heart liquid as water – "O Lord, revive thy work." Sometimes this feeling is very deep; persons have been bowed down, so that they could neither stand nor sit. I can name men in this state, of firm nerves, who stand high in character, who have been absolutely crushed with grief for the state of sinners. They have had an actual travail of soul for sinners, till they were as helpless as children. The feeling is not always so great as this, but such things are much more common than is supposed. In the great revivals in 1826, they were common. This is by no means enthusiasm. It is just what Paul felt, when he says, "My little children, of whom I travail in birth." I heard of a person in this State, who prayed for sinners, and finally got into such a state of mind, that she could not live without prayer. She could not rest day nor night, unless there was somebody praying. Then she would be at ease; but if they ceased, she would shriek in agony till there was prayer again. And this continued for two days, until she prevailed in prayer, and her soul was relieved. This travail of soul, is that deep agony, which persons feel when they lay hold on God for such a blessing, and will not let him go till they receive it. I do not mean to be understood that it is essential to a spirit of prayer, that the distress should be so great as this. But this deep, continual, earnest desire for the salvation of sinners, is what constitutes the spirit of prayer for a revival. It is a revival begun so far as this spirit of prayer extends.

When this feeling exists in a church, unless the Spirit is grieved away by sin, there will infallibly be a revival of Christians generally, and it will involve the conversion of sinners to God. This anxiety and distress increases till the revival commences. A clergyman in W----n told me of a revival among his people, which commenced with a zealous and devoted woman in the church. She became anxious about sinners, and went to praying for them, and she prayed and her distress increased; and she finally came to her minister, and talked with him, and asked him to appoint an anxious meeting, for she felt that one was needed. The minister put her off, for he felt nothing of it. The next week she came again, and besought him to appoint an anxious meeting; she knew there would be somebody to come, for she felt as if God was going to pour out his Spirit. He put her off again. And finally she said to him, "If you do not appoint an anxious meeting I shall die, for there is certainly going to be a revival." The next Sabbath he appointed a meeting, and said that if there were any who wished to converse with him about the salvation of their souls, he would meet them on such an evening. He did not know of one, but when he went to the place, to his astonishment he found a large number of anxious inquirers. Now do not you think that woman knew there was going to be a revival? Call it what you please, a new revelation, or an old revelation, or anything else. I say it was the Spirit of God that taught that praying woman there was going to be a revival. "The secret of the Lord" was with her, and she knew it. She knew God had been in her heart, and filled it so full that she could contain no longer.

Sometimes ministers have had this distress about their congregations, so that they felt as if they could not live unless they could see a revival. Sometimes elders and deacons, or private members of the church, men or women, have the spirit of prayer for a revival of religion, so that they will hold on and prevail with God, till he pours out his Spirit. The first ray of light that broke in upon the midnight which rested on the churches in Oneida county, in the fall of 1825, was from a woman in feeble health, who, I believe, had never been in a powerful revival. Her soul was exercised about sinners. She was in an agony for the land. She did not know what ailed her, but she kept praying more and more, till it seemed as if her agony would destroy her body. At length she became full of joy, and exclaimed, "God has come! God has come! There is no mistake about it, the work is begun, and is going over all the region." And sure enough, the work began, and her family were almost all converted, and the work spread all over that part of the country. Now, do you think that woman was deceived? I tell you, no. She knew she had prevailed with God in prayer. She had travailed in birth for souls, and she knew it. This was not the only instance, by many, that I knew in that region.

Generally, there are but few professors of religion that know anything about this spirit of prayer which prevails with God. I have been amazed to see such accounts as are often published about revivals, as if the revival had come without any cause — nobody knew why or wherefore. I have sometimes inquired into such cases; when it had been given out that nobody knew anything about it until one Sabbath they saw in the face of the congregation that God was there, or they saw it in their conference room, or prayer meeting, and were astonished at the mysterious sovereignty of God, in bringing in a revival without any apparent connection with means. Now mark me. Go and inquire among the obscure members of the church, and you will always find that somebody had been praying for a revival, and was expecting it--some man or woman had been agonizing in prayer, for the salvation of sinners, until they gained the blessing. It may have found the minister and the body of the church fast asleep, and they would wake up all of a sudden, like a man just rubbing his eyes open, and running round the room pushing things over, and wondering where all this excitement came from. But though few knew it, you may be sure there has been somebody on the watch-tower; constant in prayer till the blessing came. Generally, a revival is more or less extensive, as there are more or less persons who have the spirit of prayer. But I will not dwell on this subject any further at present, as the subject of prayer will come up again in this course of lectures.

Another sign that a revival may be expected, is *when the attention of ministers is especially directed to this particular object, and when their preaching and other efforts are aimed particularly at the conversion of sinners*. Most of the time the labors of ministers are, it would seem, directed to other objects. They seem to preach and labor with no particular design to effect the immediate conversion of sinners. And then it need not be expected that there will be a revival under their preaching. There never will be a revival till somebody makes particular efforts for this end. But when the attention of a minister is directed to the state of the families in his congregation, and his heart is full of feeling of the necessity of a revival, and when he puts forth the proper efforts for this end, then you may be prepared to expect a revival. As I explained last week, the connection between the right use of means for a revival,

When a Revival is to be Expected

and a revival, is as philosophically sure as between the right use of means to raise grain, and a crop of wheat. I believe, in fact, it is more certain, and that there are fewer instances of failure. The effect is more certain to follow. The paramount importance of spiritual things makes it reasonable that it should be so. Take the Bible, the nature of the case, and the history of the church all together, and you will find fewer failures in the use of means for a revival, than in farming, or any other worldly business. In worldly business there are sometimes cases where counteracting causes annihilate all a man can do. In raising grain, for instance, there are cases which are beyond the control of man, such as drought, hard winter, worms, and so on. So in laboring to promote a revival, there may things occur to counteract it, something or other turning up to divert the public attention from religion, which may baffle every effort. But I believe there are fewer such cases in the moral than in the natural world. I have seldom seen an individual fail, when he used the means for promoting a revival in earnest, in the manner pointed out in the word of God. I believe a man may enter on the work of promoting a revival, with as reasonable an expectation of success, as he can enter on any other work with an expectation of success; with the same expectation as the farmer has of a crop when he sows his grain. I have sometimes seen this tried and succeed under circumstances the most forbidding that can be conceived.

The great revival in Rochester began under the most disadvantageous circumstances that could well be imagined. It seemed as though Satan had interposed every possible obstacle to a revival. The three churches were at variance; one had no minister, one was divided and about to dismiss their minister. An elder of the third Presbyterian church had brought a charge of

31

unchristian conduct against the pastor of the first church, and they were just going to have a trial before the presbytery. After the work began, one of the first things was, the great stone church gave way, and created a panic. Then one of the churches went on and dismissed their minister right in the midst of it. Another church nearly broke down. Many other things occurred, so that it seemed as if the devil was determined to divert the public attention from the subject of religion. But there were a few remarkable cases of the spirit of prayer, which assured us that God was there, and we went on: and the more Satan opposed, the Spirit of the Lord lifted up the standard higher and higher, till finally a wave of salvation rolled over the place.

A revival of religion may be expected *when Christians begin to confess their sins to one another*. At other times, they confess in a general manner, as if they were only half in earnest. They may do it in eloquent language, but it does not mean anything. But when there is an ingenuous breaking down, and a pouring out of the heart in making a confession of their sins, the flood-gates will soon burst open, and salvation will flow over the place.

A revival may be expected whenever *Christians are found willing to make the sacrifice necessary to carry it on*. They must be willing to sacrifice their feelings, their business, their time, to help forward the work. Ministers must be willing to lay out their strength, and to jeopard their health and life. They must be willing to offend the impenitent by plain and faithful dealing, and perhaps offend many members of the church who will not come up to the work. They must take a decided stand with the revival, be the consequences what they may. They must be prepared to go on with the work, even though they should lose the affections of all the impenitent, and of all the cold part of the church. The minister must be prepared, if it is the will of God, to be driven away from the place. He must be determined to go straight forward, and leave the entire event with God.

I knew a minister who had a young man laboring with him in a revival. The young man preached pretty plain, and the wicked did not like him. They said, We like our minister, and we wish to have him preach. They finally said so much that the minister told the young man, "Mr. Such-a-one, that gives so much towards my support, says so and so. Mr. A. says so, and Mr. B. says so. They think it will break up the society if you continue to preach, and I think you had better not preach anymore." The young man went away, but the Spirit of God immediately withdrew from the place, and the revival stopped short. The minister, by yielding to the wicked desires of the wicked, drove him away. He was afraid the devil would drive him away from his people, and by undertaking to satisfy the devil, he offended God. And God so ordered events, that in a short time he had to leave his people after all. He undertook to go between the devil and God, and God dismissed him.

The people, also, must be willing to have a revival, let the sacrifice be what it may. It will not do for them to say, "We are willing to attend so many meetings, but we cannot attend any more." Or, "We are willing to have a revival if it will not disturb our arrangements about our business, or prevent our making money." I tell you, such people will never have a revival, till they are willing to do anything, and sacrifice anything, that God indicates to be their duty. Christian merchants must feel willing to lock up their stores for six months, if it is necessary to carry on a revival. I do not mean to say any such thing is called for, or that it is their duty to do so. But if there should be such a state of feeling as to call for it, then it would be their duty, and they ought to be willing to do it. They ought to be willing to do it if God calls, and he can easily burn down their stores if they do not. In fact, I should not be sorry to see such a revival in New York, as would make every merchant in the city lock up his store till spring, and say he had sold goods enough, and now he would give up his whole time to lead sinners to Christ.

A revival may be expected *when ministers and professors are willing to have God promote it* by what instruments he pleases. Sometimes ministers are not willing to have a revival unless they can have the management of it, or unless their agency can be conspicuous in promoting it. They wish to prescribe to God what he shall direct and bless, and what men he shall put forward. They will have no new measures. They cannot have any of this new-light preaching, or of these evangelists that go about the country preaching. They have a great deal to say about God's being a sovereign, and that he will have revivals come in his own way and time. But then he must choose to have it just in their way, or they will have nothing to do with it. Such men will sleep on till they are awakened by the judgment trumpet, without a revival, unless they are willing that God should come in his own way--unless they are willing to have anything or anybody employed, that will do the most good.

Strictly I should say that when the foregoing things occur, a revival, to the same extent, already exists. In truth a revival should be expected whenever it is needed. If we need to be revived it is our duty to be revived. If it is duty it is possible, and we should set about being revived ourselves, and, relying on the promise of Christ to be with us in making disciples always and everywhere, we ought to labor to revive Christians and convert sinners, with confident expectation of success. Therefore, whenever the church needs reviving they ought and may expect to be revived, and to see sinners converted to Christ. When those things are seen which are named under the foregoing heads, let Christians and ministers be encouraged and know that a good work is already begun. Follow it up.

Do You Truly Wish for a Revival?

Brethren, you can tell from our subject, whether you need a revival here or not, in this church, and in this city; and whether you are going to have one or not. Elders of the church, men, women, any of you, and all of you – what do you say?

Do you need a revival here?

Do you expect to have one?

Have you any reason to expect one?

You need not make any mist about it; for you know, or can know if you will, whether you have any reason to look for a revival here.

You see why you have not a revival. It is only because you do not want one. Because you are not praying for it; nor anxious for it, nor putting forth efforts for it. I appeal to your own consciences. Are you making these efforts now, to promote a revival? You know, brethren, what the truth is about it. Will you stand up and say that you have made the efforts for a revival and been disappointed – that you have cried to God, "Wilt thou not revive us?" and God would not do it?

Do you wish for a revival? Will you have one? If God should ask you this moment, by an audible voice from heaven, "Do you want a revival?" would you dare to say, Yes? "Are you willing to make the sacrifices?" would you answer, Yes? "When shall it begin?" would you answer, Let it begin tonight; let it begin here; let it begin in my heart NOW? Would you dare to say so to God, if you should hear his voice to-night?

Questions:

1. Work through each of these: Does your church need a revival? Does your group need a revival? Do you need a revival?

2. What benefits do you see in a revival?

3. What signs do you see that a revival may be expected?

Action:

Take some time to think over what sacrifices you are willing to make to see revival.

chapter three
How to Promote a Revival

*Break up your fallow ground;
for it is time to seek the LORD,
till he come and rain righteousness upon you.*

HOSEA 10:12

The Jews were a nation of farmers, and it is therefore a common thing in the Scriptures to refer for illustrations to their occupation, and to the scenes with which farmers and shepherds are familiar. The prophet Hosea addresses them as a nation of backsliders, and reproves them for their idolatry, and threatens them with the judgments of God. I have showed you in my first lecture what a revival is not, what it is, and the agencies to be employed in promoting it; and in my second, when it is needed, its importance, and when it may be expected. My design in this lecture is to show how a revival is to be promoted.

The Fallow Ground

A revival consists of two parts; as it respects the church, and as it respects the ungodly. I shall speak tonight of a revival in the church. Fallow ground is ground which has once been tilled, but which now lies waste, and needs to be broken up and mellowed, before it is suited to receive grain. I shall show, as it respects a revival in the church, what it is to break up the fallow ground, in the sense of the text, and how it is to be performed.

What is it to break up the fallow ground? To break up the fallow ground, is to break up your hearts – to prepare your minds to bring forth fruit unto God. The mind of man is often compared in the Bible to ground, and the word of God to seed sown in it, and the fruit represents the actions and affections of those who receive it. To break up the fallow ground, therefore, is to bring the mind into such a state, that it is fitted to receive the word of God. Sometimes your hearts get matted down hard and dry, and all run to waste, till there is no such thing as getting fruit from them till they are all broken up, and mellowed down, and fitted to receive the word of God. It is this softening of the heart, so as to make it feel the truth, which the prophet calls breaking up your fallow ground.

How is the fallow ground to be broken up? It is not by any direct efforts to feel. People run into a mistake on this subject, from not making the laws of mind the object of thought. There are great errors on the subject of the laws which govern the mind. People talk about religious feeling, as if they thought they could, by direct effort, call forth religious affection. But this is not the way the mind acts. No man can make himself feel in this way, merely by trying to feel. The feelings of the mind are not directly under our control. We cannot by willing, or by direct volition, call forth religious feelings. We might as well think to call spirits up from the deep. They are purely involuntary states of mind. They naturally and necessarily exist in the mind under certain circumstances calculated to excite them. But they can be controlled indirectly. Otherwise there would be no moral character in our feelings, if there were not a way to control them. We cannot say, "Now I will feel so and so towards such an object." But we can command our attention to it, and look at it intently, till the involuntary affections arise. Let a man who is away from his family, bring them up before his mind, and will he not feel? But it is not by saying to himself, "Now I will feel deeply for my family." A man can direct his attention to any object, about which he ought to feel and wishes to feel, and in that way he will call into existence the proper emotions. Let a man call up his enemy before his mind, and his feelings of enmity will rise. So if a man thinks of God, and fastens his mind on any parts of God's character, he will feel--emotions will come up, by the very laws of mind. If he is a friend of God, let him contemplate God as a gracious and holy being, and he will have emotions of friendship kindled up in his mind. If he is an enemy of God, only let him get the true character of God before his mind, and look at it, and fasten his attention on it, and his enmity will rise against God, or he will break down and give his heart to God.

If you wish to break up the fallow ground of your hearts, and make your minds feel on the subject of religion, you must go to work just as you would to feel on any other subject. Instead of keeping your thoughts on everything else, and then imagine that by going to a few meetings you will get your feelings enlisted, go the common sense way to work, as you would on any other subject. It is just as easy to make your minds feel on the subject of religion as it is on any other subject. God has put these states of mind under your control. If people were as unphilosophical about moving their limbs, as they are about regulating their emotions, you would never have got here to meeting tonight.

Breaking Fallow Ground Requires Examination

If you mean to break up the fallow ground of your hearts, you must begin by looking at your hearts – examine and note the state of your minds, and see where you are. Many never seem to think about this. They pay no attention to their own hearts, and never know whether they are doing well in religion or not – whether they are gaining ground or going back – whether they are fruitful, or lying waste like the fallow ground. Now you must draw off your attention from other things, and look into this. Make a business of it. Do not be in a hurry. Examine thoroughly the state of your hearts, and see where you are – whether you are walking with God every day, or walking with the devil – whether you are serving God or serving the devil most – whether you are under the dominion of the prince of darkness, or the Lord Jesus Christ.

To do all this, you must set yourself at work to consider your sins. You must examine yourselves. And by this I do not mean, that you must stop and look directly within to see what is the present state of your feelings. That is the very way to put a stop to all feeling. This is just as absurd as it would be for a man to shut his eyes on the lamp, and try to turn his eyes inward to find out whether there was any image painted on the retina. The man complains that he does not see anything! And why? Because he has turned his eyes away from the objects of sight. The truth is, our moral feelings are as much an object of consciousness as our sensations. And the way to excite is to go on acting, and employing our minds. Then we can tell our moral feelings by consciousness, just as I could tell my natural feelings by consciousness, if I should put my hand in the fire.

Self-examination consists in looking at your lives, in considering your actions, in calling up the past, and learning its true character. Look back over your past history. Take up your individual sins one by one, and look at them. I do not mean that you should just cast a glance at your past life, and see that it has been full of sins, and then go to God and make a sort of general confession, and ask for pardon. That is not the way. You must take them up one by one. It will be a good thing to take a pen and paper, as you go over them, and write them down as they occur to you. Go over them as carefully as a merchant goes over his books; and as often as a sin comes before your memory, add it to the list. General confessions of sin will never do. Your sins were committed one by one; and as far as you can come at them, they ought to be reviewed and repented of one by one.

Now begin; and take up first what are commonly, but improperly, called your **sins of omission**.

Ingratitude. Take this sin, for instance, and write down under it all the instances you can remember, wherein you have received favors from God, for which you have never exercised gratitude. How many cases can you remember? Some remarkable providence, some wonderful turn of events, that saved you from ruin. Set down the instances of God's goodness to you when you were in sin, before your conversion. Then the mercy of God in the circumstances of your conversion, for which you have never been half thankful enough. The numerous mercies you have received since. How long the catalogue of instances, where your ingratitude is so black that you are forced to hide your face in confusion! Now go on your knees, and confess them one by one to God, and ask forgiveness. The very act of confession, by the laws of suggestion, will bring up others to your memory. Put down these. Go over these three or four times in this way, and you will find an astonishing amount of mercies, for which you have never thanked God.

Then take another sin. Let it be, *want of love to God*. Write that down, and go over all the instances you can remember, when you did not give to the blessed God that hearty love which you ought.

Think how grieved and alarmed you would be, if you discovered any flagging of affection for you in your wife, husband, or children; if you saw somebody else engrossing their hearts, and thoughts, and time. Perhaps, in such a case, you would well nigh die with a just and virtuous jealousy. Now, God styles himself a jealous God; and have you not given your heart to other loves: played the harlot, and infinitely offended him?

Neglect of the Bible. Put down the cases, when for days, and perhaps for weeks – yea, it may be, even for months together, you had no pleasure in God's word. Perhaps you did not read a chapter, or if you read it, it was in a way that was still more displeasing to God. Many people read over a whole chapter in such a way, that if they were put under oath when they have done, they could not tell what they have been reading. With so little attention do they read, that they cannot remember where they have read from morning till evening, unless they put in a string or turn down a leaf. This demonstrates that they did not lay to heart what they read, that they did not make it a subject of reflection. If you were reading a novel, or any other piece of intelligence that greatly interested you, would you not remember what you read last? And the fact that you fold a leaf or put in a string, demonstrates that you read rather as a task, than from love or reverence for the word of God. The word of God is the rule of your duty. And do you pay so little regard to it as not to remember what you read? If so, no wonder that you live so at random, and that your religion is such a miserable failure.

Unbelief. Instances in which you have virtually charged the God of truth with lying, by your unbelief of his express promises and declarations. God has promised to give the Holy Spirit to them that ask him. Now, have you believed this? Have you expected him to answer? Have you not virtually said in your hearts, when you prayed for the Holy Spirit, "I do not believe that I shall receive it?" If you have not believed nor expected you should receive the blessing, which God has expressly promised, you have charged him with lying.

Neglect of prayer. Times when you omitted secret prayer, family prayer, and prayer meetings, or have prayed in such a way as more grievously to offend God, than to have neglected it altogether.

Neglect of the means of grace. When you have suffered trifling excuses to prevent your attending meetings, have neglected and poured contempt upon the means of salvation, merely from disrelish of spiritual duties.

The manner in which you have performed those duties – want of feeling – want of faith – worldly frame of mind – so that your words were nothing but the mere chattering of a wretch, that did not deserve that God should feel the least care for him. When you have fallen down upon your knees, and said your prayers, in such an unfeeling and careless manner, that if you had been put under oath five minutes after you left your closet, you could not have told what you had been praying for.

Your want of love for the souls of your fellow-men. Look round upon your friends and relations, and remember how little compassion you have felt for them. You have stood by and seen them going right to hell, and it seems as though you did not care if they did. How many days have there been, in which you did not make their condition the subject of a single fervent prayer, or even an ardent desire for their salvation?

Your want of care for the heathen. Perhaps you have not cared enough for them to attempt to learn their condition; perhaps not even to take a Missionary paper. Look at this, and see how much you do really care for the heathen, and set down honestly the real amount of your feelings for them, and your desire for their salvation. Measure your desire for their salvation by the self-denial you practise, in giving of your substance to send them the Gospel. Do you deny yourself even the hurtful superfluities of life, such as tea, coffee, and tobacco? Do you retrench your style of living, and really subject yourself to any inconvenience to save them? Do you daily pray for them in your closet? Do you statedly attend the monthly concert? Are you from month to month laying by something to put into the treasury of the Lord, when you go up to pray? If you are not doing these things, and if your soul is not agonized for the poor benighted heathen, why are you such a hypocrite as to pretend to be a Christian? Why, your profession is an insult to Jesus Christ!

Your neglect of family duties. How you have lived before them, how you have prayed, what an example you have set before them. What direct efforts do you habitually make for their spiritual good? What duty have you not neglected?

Neglect of social duties.

Neglect of watchfulness over your own life. Instances in which you have hurried over your private duties, and not taken yourself to task, nor honestly made up your accounts with God. Where you have entirely neglected to watch your conduct, and have been off your guard, and have sinned before the world, and before the church, and before God.

Neglect to watch over your brethren. How often have you broken your covenant, that you would watch over them in the Lord! How little do you know or care about the state of their souls! And yet you are under a solemn oath to watch over them. What have you done to make yourself acquainted with them? How many of them have you interested yourself for, to know their spiritual state? Go over the list, and wherever you find there has been a neglect, write it down. How many times have you seen your brethren growing cold in religion, and have not spoken to them about it? You have seen them beginning to neglect one duty after another, and you did not reprove them in a brotherly way. You have seen them falling into sin, and you let them go on. And yet you pretend to love them. What a hypocrite! Would you see your wife or child going into disgrace, or into the fire, and hold your peace? No, you would not. What do you think of yourself, then, to pretend to love Christians, and to love Christ, while you can see them going into disgrace, and say nothing to them?

Neglect of self-denial. There are many professors who are willing to do almost anything in religion, that does not require self-denial. But when they are called to do anything that requires them to deny themselves, Oh that is too much! They think they are doing a great deal for God, and doing about as much as he ought to ask in reason, if they are only doing what they can do about as well as not; but they are not willing to deny themselves any comfort or convenience whatever, for the sake of serving the Lord. They will not willingly suffer reproach for the name of Christ. Nor will they deny themselves the luxuries of life, to save a world from hell. So far are they from remembering that self-denial is a condition of discipleship, that they do not know what self-denial is. They never have really denied themselves a riband or a pin for Christ, and for the Gospel. Oh, how soon such professors will be in hell! Some are giving of their abundance, and are giving much, and are ready to complain that others don't give more; when, in truth, they do not give any thing that they need, anything that they could enjoy, if they kept it. They only give of their surplus wealth; and perhaps that poor woman, who puts in twelve and a half cents at the monthly concert, has exercised more self-denial, than they have in giving thousands.

* * *

From these we now turn to **sins of commission**.

Worldly mindedness. What has been the state of your heart in regard to your worldly possessions? Have you looked at them as really yours – as if you had a right to dispose of them as your own, according to your own will? If you have, write that down. If you have loved property, and sought after it for its own sake, or to gratify lust or ambition, or a worldly spirit, or to lay it up for your families, you have sinned, and must repent.

Pride. Recollect all the instances you can, in which you have detected yourself in the exercise of pride. Vanity is a particular form of pride. How many times have you detected yourself in consulting vanity, about your dress and appearance? How many times have you thought more, and taken more pains, and spent more time, about decorating your body to go to church, than you have about preparing your mind for the worship of God? You have gone to the house of God caring more how you appear outwardly in the sight of mortal men, than how your soul appears in the sight of the heart-searching God. You have in fact set up yourself to be worshipped by them, rather than prepared to worship God yourself. You came to divide the worship of God's house, to draw off the attention of God's people to look at your pretty appearance. It is in vain to pretend now, that you don't care anything about having people look at you. Be honest about it. Would you take all this pains about your looks if everybody was blind?

Envy. Look at the cases in which you were envious at those who you thought were above you in any respect. Or perhaps you have envied those who have been more talented or more useful than yourself. Have you not so envied some, that you have been pained to hear them praised? It has been more agreeable to you to dwell upon their faults, than upon their virtues, upon their failures, than upon their success. Be honest with yourself, and if you have harbored this spirit of hell, repent deeply before God, or he will never forgive you.

Censoriousness. Instances in which you have had a bitter spirit, and spoken of Christians in a manner entirely devoid of charity and love – charity, which requires you always to hope the best the case will admit, and to put the best construction upon any ambiguous conduct.

Slander. The times you have spoken behind people's backs of their faults, real or supposed, of members of the church or others, unnecessarily or without good reason. This is slander. You need not lie to be guilty of slander; to tell the truth with the design to injure, is slander.

Levity. How often have you trifled before God, as you would not have dared to trifle in the presence of an earthly sovereign? You have either been an Atheist, and forgotten that there was a God, or have had less respect for him, and his presence, than you would have had for an earthly judge.

Lying. Understand now what lying is. Any species of designed deception for a selfish reason is lying. If the deception is not a design it is not lying. But if you design to make an impression contrary to the naked truth, you lie. Put down all those cases you can recollect. Don't call them by any soft name. God calls them LIES, and charges you with LYING, and you had better charge yourself correctly.

How innumerable are the falsehoods perpetrated every day in business, and in social intercourse, by words, and looks, and actions – designed to make an impression on others contrary to the truth for selfish reasons.

Cheating. Set down all the cases in which you have dealt with an individual, and done to him that which you would not like to have done to you. That is cheating. God has laid down a rule in the case; "All things whatsoever ye would that men should do to you, do ye even so to them." That is the rule; and now if you have not done so you are a cheat. Mind, the rule is not that you should do what you might reasonably expect them to do to you. That is a rule which would admit of every degree of wickedness. But it is "As ye WOULD they should do to you."

Hypocrisy. For instance, in your prayers and confessions to God. Set down the instances in which you have prayed for things you did not really want. And the evidence is, that when you had done praying, you could not tell what you had prayed for. How many times have you confessed sins that you did not mean to break off, and when you had no solemn purpose not to repeat them? Yes, have confessed sins when you knew you as much expected to go and repeat them as you expected to live.

Robbing God. Instances in which you have misspent your time, and squandered hours which God gave you to serve him and save souls, in vain amusements or foolish conversation, reading novels, or doing nothing; cases where you have misapplied your talents and powers of mind; where you have squandered money on your lusts, or spent it for things you did not need, and which neither contributed to your health, comfort or usefulness. Perhaps some of you who are here to-night have laid out God's money for TOBACCO. I will not speak of rum, for I presume there is no professor of religion here tonight that would drink rum. I hope there is no one that uses that filthy poison, tobacco. Think of a professor of religion, using God's money to poison himself with tobacco!

Bad temper. Perhaps you have abused your wife, or your children, or your family, or servants, or neighbors. Write it all down.

Hindering others from being useful. Perhaps you have weakened their influence by insinuations against them. You have not only robbed God of your own talents, but tied the hands of somebody else. What a wicked servant is he that loiters himself, and hinders the rest! This is done sometimes by taking their time needlessly; sometimes by destroying Christian confidence in them. Thus you have played into the hands of Satan, and not only showed yourself an idle vagabond, but prevented others from working.

* * *

Deal At Once with Your Sins

If you find you have committed a fault against an individual, and that individual is within your reach, go and confess it immediately, and get that out of the way. If the individual you have injured is too far off for you to go and see him, sit down and write him a letter, and confess the injury, pay the postage, and put it into the mail immediately. I say, pay the postage, or otherwise you will only make the matter worse. You will add to the former injury, by making him a bill of expense. The man that writes a letter on his own business, and sends it to another without paying the postage, is dishonest, and has cheated him out of so much. And if he would cheat a man out of a sixpence or shilling, when the temptation is so small, what would he not do were the temptation greater, if he had the prospect of impunity? If you have defrauded anybody, send the money, the full amount and the interest.

Go thoroughly to work in all this. Go now. Don't put it off; that will only make the matter worse. Confess to God those sins that have been committed against God, and to man those sins that have been committed against man. Don't think of getting off by going round the stumbling blocks. Take them up out of the way. In breaking up your fallow ground, you must remove every obstruction. Things may be left that you may think little things, and you may wonder why you do not feel as you wish to in religion, when the reason is that your proud and carnal mind has covered up something which God required you to confess and remove. Break up all the ground and turn it over. Do not balk it, as the farmers say; do not turn aside for little difficulties; drive the plow right through them, beam deep, and turn the ground all up, so that it may all be mellow and soft, and fit to receive the seed and bear fruit a hundred fold.

When you have gone over your whole history in this way, thoroughly, if you will then go over the ground the second time, and give your solemn and fixed attention to it, you will find that the things you have put down will suggest other things of which you have been guilty, connected with them, or near them. Then go over it a third time, and you will recollect other things connected with these. And you will find in the end that you can remember an amount of your history, and particular actions, even in this life, which you did not think you should remember in eternity. Unless you do take up your sins in this way, and consider them in detail, one by one, you can form no idea of the amount of your sins. You should go over it as thoroughly and as carefully, and as solemnly, as you would if you were just preparing yourself for the judgment.

As you go over the catalogue of your sins, be sure to resolve upon present and entire reformation. Wherever you find anything wrong, resolve at once, in the strength of God, to sin no more in that way. It will be of no benefit to examine yourself, unless you determine to amend in every particular that you find wrong in heart, temper, or conduct.

If you find, as you go on with this duty, that your mind is still all dark, cast about you, and you will find there is some reason for the Spirit of God to depart from you. You have not been faithful and thorough. In the progress of such a work you have got to do violence to yourself, and bring yourself as a rational being up to this work, with the Bible before you, and try your heart till you do feel. You need not expect that God will work a miracle for you to break up your fallow ground. It is to be done by means. Fasten your attention to the subject of your sins. You cannot look at your sins long and thoroughly, and see how bad they are, without feeling, and feeling deeply. Experience abundantly proves the benefit of going over our history in this way. Set yourself to the work now; resolve that you never will stop till you find you can pray. You never will have the spirit of prayer, till you examine yourself, and confess your sins, and break up your fallow ground. You never will have the Spirit of God dwelling in you, till you have unraveled this whole mystery of iniquity, and spread out your sins before God. Let there be this deep work of repentance, and full confession, this breaking down before God, and you will have as much of the spirit of prayer as your body can bear up under. The reason why so few Christians know anything about the spirit of prayer, is because they never would take the pains to examine themselves properly, and so never knew what it was to have their hearts all broken up in this way.

You see I have only begun to lay open this subject tonight. I want to lay it out before you, in the course of these lectures, so that if you will begin and go on to do as I say, the results will be just as certain as they are when the farmer breaks up a fallow field, and mellows it, and sows his grain. It will be so, if you will only begin in this way, and hold on till all your hardened and callous hearts break up.

The Difficulty of Unbroken Ground

It will do no good to preach to you while your hearts are in this hardened, and waste, and fallow state. The farmer might just as well sow his grain on the rock. It will bring forth no fruit. This is the reason why there are so many fruitless professors in the church, and why there is so much outside machinery, and so little deep-toned feeling in the church. Look at the Sabbath-school for instance, and see how much machinery there is, and how little of the power of godliness. If you go on in this way, the word of God will continue to harden you, and you will grow worse and worse, just as the rain and snow on an old fallow field makes the turf thicker, and the clods stronger.

See why so much preaching is wasted, and worse than wasted. It is because the church will not break up their fallow ground. A preacher may wear out his life, and do very little good, while there are so many stony-ground hearers, who have never had their fallow ground broken up. They are only half converted, and their religion is rather a change of opinion than a change of the feeling of their hearts. There is mechanical religion enough, but very little that looks like deep heart-work.

Professors of religion should never satisfy themselves, or expect a revival, just by starting out of their slumbers, and blustering about, and making a noise, and talking to sinners. They must get their fallow ground broken up. It is utterly unphilosophical to think of getting engaged in religion in this way. If your fallow ground is broken up, then the way to get more feeling, is to go out and see sinners on the road to hell, and talk to them, and guide inquiring souls, and you will get more feeling. You may get into an excitement without this breaking up; you may show a kind of zeal, but it will not last long, and it will not take hold of sinners, unless your hearts are broken up. The reason is, that you go about it mechanically, and have not broken up your fallow ground.

And now, finally, will you break up your fallow ground? Will you enter upon the course now pointed out, and persevere till you are thoroughly awake? If you fail here, if you do not do this, and get prepared, you can go no further with me in this course of lectures. I have gone with you as far as it is of any use to go, until your fallow ground is broken up. Now, you must make thorough work upon this point, or all I have further to say will do you little good. Nay, it will only harden and make you worse. If, when next Friday night arrives, it finds you with unbroken hearts, you need not expect to be benefited by what I shall say. If you do not set about this work immediately, I shall take it for granted that you do not mean to be revived, that you have forsaken your minister, and mean to let him go up to battle alone. If you do not do this, I charge you with having forsaken Christ, with refusing to repent and do your first work. But if you will be prepared to enter upon the work, I propose, God willing, next Friday evening, to lead you into the work of saving sinners.

Questions:

1. What keeps Christians from dealing with their sin in an honest way?

2. When have you taken time to examine your heart like Finney describes? What was the result?

3. Which of the list of sins (Omission or Commission) challenges you the most and why?

Action:

Take some time to work through the lists and deal with your own heart, and if you need to make things right do so as soon as possible.

chapter four
Prevailing Prayer

> *The effectual, fervent prayer*
> *of a righteous man availeth much.*
>
> JAMES 5:16

The last lecture referred principally to the confession of sin. To-night my remarks will be chiefly confined to the subject of intercession, or prayer. There are two kinds of means requisite to promote a revival; one to influence men, the other to influence God. The truth is employed to influence men, and prayer to move God. When I speak of moving God, I do not mean that God's mind is changed by prayer, or that his disposition or character is changed. But prayer produces such a change in us and fulfils such conditions as renders it consistent for God to do as it would not be consistent for him to do otherwise. When a sinner repents, that state of mind makes it proper for God to forgive him. God has always been ready to forgive him on that condition, so that when the sinner changes his mind towards God, it requires no change of feeling in God to pardon him. It is the sinner's repentance that renders his forgiveness proper, and is the occasion of God's acting as he does. So when Christians offer effectual prayer, their state of mind renders it proper for God to answer them. He was always ready to bestow the blessing, on the condition that they felt right, and offered the right kind of prayer. Whenever this change takes place in them, and they offer the right kind of prayer, then God, without any change in himself, can answer them. When we offer effectual fervent prayer for others, the fact that we offer such prayer renders it consistent for him to do what we pray for, when otherwise it would not have been consistent.

Prayer is an essential link in the chain of causes that lead to a revival; as much so as truth is. Some have zealously used truth to convert men, and laid very little stress on prayer. They have preached, and talked, and distributed tracts with great zeal, and then wondered that they had so little success. And the reason was, that they forgot to use the other branch of the means, effectual prayer. They overlooked the fact, that truth by itself will never produce the effect, without the Spirit of God, and that Spirit is given in answer to earnest prayer.

Sometimes it happens that those who are the most engaged in employing truth, are not the most engaged in prayer. This is always unhappy. For unless they, or somebody else have the spirit of prayer, the truth by itself will do nothing but harden men in impenitence. Probably in the day of judgment it will be found that nothing is ever done by the truth, used ever so zealously, unless there is a spirit of prayer somewhere in connection with the presentation of truth.

Others err on the other side. Not that they lay too much stress on prayer. But they overlook the fact that prayer might be offered for ever, by itself, and nothing would be done. Because sinners are not converted by direct contact of the Holy Ghost, but by the truth, employed as a means. To expect the conversion of sinners by prayer alone, without the employment of truth, is to tempt God.

The subject of discourse this evening, is prevailing prayer. I propose to show what is effectual or prevailing prayer, state some of the most essential attributes of prevailing prayer, give some reasons why God requires this kind of prayer, and to show that such prayer will avail much.

What is Prevailing Prayer?

Effectual, prevailing prayer, does not consist in benevolent desires merely. Benevolent desires are doubtless pleasing to God. Such desires pervade heaven, and are found in all holy beings. But they are not prayer. Men may have these desires as the angels and glorified spirits have them. But this is not the effectual, prevailing prayer, spoken of in the text. Prevailing prayer is something more than this.

Prevailing, or effectual prayer, is *that prayer which obtains the blessing that it seeks*. It is that prayer which effectually moves God. The very idea of effectual prayer is, that it effects its object.

Attributes of Prevailing Prayer

I will state some of the most essential attributes of prevailing prayer. I cannot detail in full all the things that go to make up prevailing prayer. But I will mention some things that are essential to it; some things which a person must do in order to prevail in prayer.

He must pray for a definite object. He need not expect to offer such prayer, if he prays at random, without any distinct or definite object. He must have an object distinctly before his mind. I speak now of secret prayer. Many people go away into their closets, because they must say their prayers. The time has come that they are in the habit of going by themselves for prayer, in the morning, or at noon, or at whatever time of day it may be. And instead of having anything to say, any definite object before their mind, they fall down on their knees, and pray for just what comes into their minds, for everything that floats in their imagination at the time, and when they have done, they could not tell hardly a word of what they have been praying for. This is not effectual prayer. What should we think of anybody who should try to move a legislature so, and should say, "Now it is winter, and the legislature is in session, and it is time to send up petitions," and should go up to the legislature and petition at random, without any definite object? Do you think such petitions would move the legislature?

A man must have some definite object before his mind. He cannot pray effectually for a variety of objects at once. The mind of man is so constituted that it cannot fasten its desires intensely upon many things at the same time. All the instances of effectual prayer recorded in the Bible were of this kind. Wherever you see that the blessing sought for in prayer was attained, you will find that the prayer which was offered was prayer for that definite object.

Prayer, to be effectual, *must be in accordance with the revealed will of God*. To pray for things contrary to the revealed will of God, is to tempt God.

There are three ways in which God's will is revealed to men for their guidance in prayer.

(1) By express promises or predictions in the Bible, that he will give or do certain things. Either by express promises in regard to particular things, or promises in general terms, so that we may apply them to particular things. For instance, there is this promise: "Whatsoever things ye desire, when ye pray, believe that ye receive them, and ye shall have them."

(2) Sometimes God reveals his will by his providence. When he makes it clear that such and such events are about to take place, it is as much a revelation as if he had written it in his word. It would be impossible to reveal everything in the Bible. But God often makes it clear to those who have spiritual discernment, that it is his will to grant such and such blessings.

(3) By his Spirit. When God's people are at a loss what to pray for, agreeable to his will, his Spirit often instructs them. Where there is no particular revelation, and providence leaves it dark, and we know not what to pray for as we ought, we are expressly told, that "the Spirit also helpeth our infirmities," and "the Spirit itself maketh intercession for us with groanings that cannot be uttered." A great deal has been said on the subject of praying in faith for things not revealed. It is objected, that this doctrine implies a new revelation. I answer, that, new or old, it is the very revelation that Jehovah says he makes. It is just as plain here, as if it were now revealed by a voice from heaven, that the Spirit of God helps the people of God to pray according to the will of God, when they themselves know not what things they ought to pray for. "And he that searcheth the heart knoweth the mind of the Spirit," because he maketh intercession for the saints according to the will of God, and he leads Christians to pray for just those things, with

groanings that cannot be uttered. When neither the word nor providence enables them to decide, then let them be filled with the Spirit, as God commands them to be. He says, "Be ye filled with the Spirit." And He will lead their mind to such things as God is willing to grant.

To pray effectually, *you must pray with submission to the will of God*. Do not confound submission with indifference. No two things are more unlike. I once knew an individual come where there was a revival. He himself was cold, and did not enter into the spirit of it, and had no spirit of prayer; and when he heard the brethren pray as if they could not be denied, he was shocked at their boldness, and kept all the time insisting on the importance of praying with submission; when it was as plain as anything could be, that he confounded submission with indifference

So again, do not confound submission in prayer with a general confidence that God will do what is right. It is proper to have this confidence that God will do what is right in all things. But this is a different thing from submission. What I mean by submission in prayer, is, acquiescence in the revealed will of God. To submit to any command of God is to obey it. Submission to some supposable or possible, but secret decree of God, is not submission. To submit to any dispensation of Providence is impossible till it comes. For we never can know what the event is to be, till it takes place. Take a case: David, when his child was sick, was distressed, and agonized in prayer, and refused to be comforted. He took it so much to heart, that when the child died, his servants were afraid to tell him the child was dead, for fear he would vex himself still worse. But as soon as he heard that the child was dead, he laid aside his grief, and arose, and asked for food, and ate and drank as usual. While the child was yet alive, he did not know what was the will of God, and so he fasted and prayed, and said, "Who can tell whether God will be gracious to me, that my child may live?" He did not know but that his prayer and agony was the very thing on which it turned, whether the child was to live or not. He thought that if he humbled himself and entreated God, perhaps God would spare him this blow. But as soon as God's will appeared, and the child was dead, he bowed like a saint. He seemed not only to acquiesce, but actually to take a satisfaction in it. "I shall go to him, but he shall not return to me." This was true submission. He reasoned correctly in the case. While he had no revelation of the will of God, he did not know but what the child's recovery depended on his prayer. But when he had a revelation of the will of God, he submitted. While the will of God is not known, to submit, without prayer, is tempting God. Perhaps, and for aught you know, the fact of your offering the right kind of prayer, may be the thing on which the event turns. In the case of an impenitent friend, the very condition on which he is to be saved from hell, may be the fervency and importunity of your prayer for that individual.

Effectual prayer for an object implies *a desire for that object commensurate with its importance*. If a person truly desires any blessing, his desires will bear some proportion to the greatness of the blessing. The desires of the Lord Jesus Christ for the blessing he prayed for, were amazingly strong, and amounted even to agony. If the desire for an object is strong, and is a benevolent desire, and the thing not contrary to the will and providence of God, the presumption is, that it will be granted. There are two reasons for this presumption.

(1) From the general benevolence of God. If it is a desirable object; if, so far as we can see, it would be an act of benevolence

in God to grant it, his general benevolence is presumptive evidence that he will grant it.

(2) If you find yourself exercised with benevolent desires for any object, there is a strong presumption that the Spirit of God is exciting these very desires, and stirring you up to pray for that object, so that it may be granted in answer to prayer. In such a case no degree of desire or importunity in prayer is improper. A Christian may come up, as it were, and take hold of the hand of God. See the case of Jacob, when he exclaimed, in an agony of desire, "I will not let thee go, except thou bless me." Was God displeased with his boldness and importunity? Not at all; but he granted him the very thing he prayed for. So in the case of Moses. God said to Moses, "Let me alone, that I may destroy them, and blot out their name from under heaven, and I will make of thee a nation mightier and greater than they." What did Moses do? Did he stand aside and let God do as he said? No, his mind runs back to the Egyptians, and he thinks how they will triumph. "Wherefore should the Egyptians say, For mischief did he bring them out." It seemed as if he took hold of the uplifted hand of God, to avert the blow. Did God rebuke him for his interference, and tell him he had no business to interfere? No; it seemed as if he was unable to deny any thing to such importunity, and so Moses stood in the gap, and prevailed with God.

It is said of Xavier, the missionary, that he was once called to pray for a man who was sick, and he prayed so fervently that he seemed as it were to do violence to heaven — so the writer expresses it. And he prevailed, and the man recovered.

Such prayer is often offered in the present day, when Christians have been wrought up to such a pitch of importunity and such a holy boldness, that afterwards, when they looked back upon it, they were frightened and amazed at themselves, to think they should dare to exercise such importunity with God. And yet these prayers have prevailed, and obtained the blessing. And many of these persons, that I am acquainted with, are among the holiest persons I know in the world.

Prayer, to be effectual, must be *offered from right motives*. Prayer should not be selfish, but dictated by a supreme regard for the glory of God. A great deal of prayer is offered from pure selfishness. Women sometimes pray for their husbands, that they may be converted, because they say, "It would be so much more pleasant to have my husband go to meeting with me," and all that. And they seem never to lift up their thoughts above self at all. They do not seem to think how their husbands are dishonoring God by their sins, and how God would be glorified in their conversion. So it is with parents very often. They cannot bear to think that their children should be lost. They pray for them very earnestly indeed. But if you go to talk with them, they are very tender, and tell you how good their children are, how they respect religion, and they think they are almost Christians now; and so they talk as if they were afraid you would hurt their children if you should tell them the truth. They do not think how such amiable and lovely children are dishonoring God by their sins; they are only thinking what a dreadful thing it will be for them to go to hell. Ah! unless their thoughts rise higher than this, their prayers will never prevail with a holy God. The temptation to selfish motives is so strong, that there is reason to fear a great many parental prayers never rise above the yearnings of parental tenderness. And that is the reason why so many prayers are not heard, and why so many pious, praying parents have ungodly children. Much of the prayer for the heathen world seems to be based on no higher principle than sympathy. Missionary agents, and others, are dwelling almost exclusively upon the six hundred millions of heathens going to hell, while little is said of their dishonoring God. This is a great evil; and until the church have higher motives for prayer and missionary effort than sympathy for the heathen, their prayers and efforts will never amount to much.

Prayer, to be effectual, *must be by the intercession of the Spirit*. You never can expect to offer prayer according to the will of God without the Spirit. In the first two cases, it is not because Christians are unable to offer such prayer, where the will of God is revealed in his word, or indicated by his providence. They are able to do it, just as they are able to be holy. But the fact is, that they are so wicked, that they never do offer such prayer, without they are influenced by the Spirit of God. There must be a faith, such as produced by the effectual operation of the Holy Ghost.

It must be persevering prayer. As a general thing, Christians who have backslidden and lost the spirit of prayer, will not get at once into the habit of persevering prayer. Their minds are not in a right state, and they cannot fix their minds, and hold on till the blessing comes. If their minds were in that state, that they would persevere till the answer comes, effectual prayer might be offered at once, as well as after praying ever so many times for an object. But they have to pray again and again, because their thoughts are so apt to wander away, and are so easily diverted from the object to something else. Until their minds get imbued with the spirit of prayer, they will not keep fixed to one point, and push their petition to an issue on the spot. Do not think you are prepared to offer prevailing prayer, if your feelings will let you pray once for an object, and then leave it. Most Christians come up to prevailing prayer by a protracted process. Their minds gradually become filled with anxiety about an object, so that they will even go about their business, sighing out their desires to God. Just as the mother whose child is sick, goes round her house, sighing as if her heart would break. And if she is a praying mother, her sighs are breathed out to God all the day long. If she goes out of the room where her child is, her mind is still on it; and if she is asleep, still her thoughts are on it, and she starts in her dreams, thinking it is dying. Her whole mind is absorbed in that sick child. This is the state of mind in which Christians offer prevailing prayer. What was the reason that Jacob wrestled all night in prayer with God? He knew that he had done his brother Esau a great injury, in getting away the birthright a long time ago. And now he was informed that his injured brother was coming to meet him, with an armed force altogether too powerful for him to contend against. And there was great reason to suppose he was coming with a purpose of revenge. There were two reasons then why he should be distressed. The first was, that he had done this great injury, and had never made any reparation. The other was, that Esau was coming with a force sufficient to crush him. Now, what does he do? Why, he first arranges everything in the best manner he can to meet his brother, sending his present first, then his property, then his family, putting those he loved most farthest behind. And by this time his mind was so exercised that he could not contain himself. He goes away alone over the brook, and pours out his very soul in an agony of prayer all night. And just as the day was breaking, the angel of the covenant said, "Let me go;" and his whole being was, as it were, agonized at the thought of giving up, and he cried out, "I will not let thee go except thou bless me." His soul was wrought up into an agony, and he obtained the blessing, but he always bore the marks of it, and showed that his body had been greatly affected by this mental struggle. This is prevailing prayer.

Now, do not deceive yourselves with thinking that you offer effectual prayer, unless you have this intense desire for the blessing. I do not believe in it. Prayer is not effectual unless it is offered up with an agony of desire. The apostle Paul speaks of it as a travail of the soul. Jesus Christ, when he was praying in the garden, was in such an agony, that he sweat as it were great drops of blood falling down to the ground. I have never known a person sweat blood; but I have known a person pray till the blood started from the nose. And I have known persons pray till they were all wet with perspiration, in the coldest weather in winter. I have known persons pray for hours, till their strength was all exhausted with the agony of their minds. Such prayers prevailed with God.

If you mean to pray effectually, *you must pray a great deal.* It was said of the apostle James, that after he was dead it was found his knees were callous like a camel's knees, by praying so much. Ah! Here was the secret of the success of those primitive ministers. They had callous knees.

If you intend prayer to be effectual, *it must be offered in the name of Christ.* You cannot come to God in your own name. You cannot plead your own merits. But you can come in a name that is always acceptable. You all know what it is to use the name of a man. If you should go to the bank with a draft or note, endorsed by John Jacob Astor, that would be giving you his name, and you know you could get the money from the bank just as well as he could himself. Now, Jesus Christ gives you the use of his name. And when you pray in the name of Christ, the meaning of it is, that you can prevail just as well as he could himself, and receive just as much as God's well-beloved Son would if he were to pray himself for the same things. But you must pray in faith. His name has all the virtue in your lips that it has in his own, and God is just as free to bestow blessings upon you, when you ask in the name of Christ, and in faith, as he would be to bestow them upon Christ, if he should ask.

You cannot prevail in prayer, without renouncing all your sins. You must not only recall them to mind, but you must actually renounce them, and leave them off, and in the purpose of your heart renounce them all forever.

You must pray in faith. You must expect to obtain the things you ask for. You need not look for an answer to prayer, if you pray without an expectation of obtaining it. You are not to form such expectations without any reason for them. In the cases I have supposed, there is a reason for the expectation. In case the thing is revealed in God's word, if you pray without an expectation of receiving the blessings, you just make God a liar. If the will of God is indicated by his providence, you ought to depend on it, according to the clearness of the indication, so far as to expect the blessing if you pray for it. And if you are led by his Spirit to pray for certain things, you have just as much reason to expect the thing to be done as if God had revealed it in his word.

But some say, "Will not this view of the leadings of the Spirit of God lead people into fanaticism?" I answer, that I know not but many may deceive themselves in respect to this matter. Multitudes have deceived themselves in regard to all the other points of religion. And if some people should think they are led by the Spirit of God, when it is nothing but their own imagination, is that any reason why those who know that they are led by the Spirit should not follow? Many people suppose themselves to be converted when they are not. Is that any reason why we should not cleave to the Lord Jesus Christ? Suppose some people are deceived in thinking they love God, is that any reason why the pious saint who knows he has the love of God shed abroad in his heart, should not give vent to his feelings in songs of praise? So I suppose some may deceive themselves in thinking they are led by the Spirit of God. But there is no need of being deceived. If people follow impulses, it is their own fault. I do not want you to follow impulses. I want you to be sober minded, and follow the sober, rational leadings of the Spirit of God. There are those who understand what I mean, and who know very well what it is to give themselves up to the Spirit of God in prayer.

Why these are Essential to Effectual Prayer

Why does God require such prayer, such strong desires, such agonizing supplications?

These strong desires strongly illustrate the strength of God's feelings. They are like the real feelings of God for impenitent sinners. When I have seen, as I sometimes have, the amazing strength of love for souls that has been felt by Christians, I have been wonderfully impressed with the amazing love of God, and his desires for their salvation. The case of a certain woman, of whom I read, in a revival, made the greatest impression on my mind. She had such an unutterable compassion and love for souls, that she actually panted for breath almost to suffocation. What must be the strength of the desire which God feels, when his Spirit produces in Christians such amazing agony, such throes of soul, such travail – God has chosen the best word to express it, it is travail, travail of the soul.

I have seen a man of as much strength of intellect and muscle as any man in the community, fall down prostrate, absolutely overpowered by his unutterable desires for sinners. I know this is a stumbling block to many; and it always will be as long as there remain in the church so many blind and stupid professors of religion. But I cannot doubt that these things are the work of the Spirit of God. Oh that the whole church could be so filled with the Spirit as to travail in prayer, till a nation should be born in a day!

These strong desires that I have described are the natural results of great benevolence and clear views of the danger of sinners. It is perfectly reasonable that it should be so. If the women who are in this house should look up there, and see a family burning to death in the fire, and hear their shrieks, and behold their agony, they would feel distressed, and it is very likely that many of them would faint away with agony. And nobody would wonder at it, or say they were fools or crazy to feel so much distressed at such an awful sight. They would think it strange if there were not some expressions of powerful feeling. Why is it any wonder, then, if Christians should feel as I have described, when they have clear views of the state of sinners, and the awful danger they are in? The fact is, that those individuals who never have felt so, have never felt much real benevolence, and their piety must be of a very superficial character. I do not mean to judge harshly, or to speak unkindly. But I state it as a simple matter of fact; and people may talk about it as they please, but I know that such piety is superficial. This is not censoriousness, but plain truth.

People sometimes wonder at Christians having such feelings. Wonder at what? Why, at the natural, and philosophical, and necessary results of deep piety towards God, and deep benevolence towards man, in view of the great danger they see sinners to be in.

The soul of a Christian, when it is thus burdened, must have relief.

God rolls this weight upon the soul of a Christian, for the purpose of bringing him near to himself. Christians are often so unbelieving, that they will not exercise proper faith in God, till he rolls this burden upon them, so heavy that they cannot live under it, and then they must go to God for relief. It is like the case of many a convicted sinner. God is willing to receive him at once, if he will come right to him, with faith in Jesus Christ. But the sinner will not come. He hangs back, and struggles, and groans under the burden of his sins, and will not throw himself upon God, till his burden of conviction becomes so great that he can live no longer; and when he is driven to desperation, as it were, and feels as if he was ready to sink into hell, he makes a mighty plunge, and throws himself upon God's mercy as his only hope. It was his duty to come before. God had no delight in his distress, for its own sake. It was only the sinner's obstinacy that created the necessity for all this distress. He would not come without it. So when professors of religion get loaded down with the weight of souls, they often pray again and again, and yet the burden is not gone, nor their distress abated, because they have never thrown it all upon God in faith. But they cannot get rid of the burden. So long as their benevolence continues it will remain and increase, and unless they resist and quench the Holy Ghost they can get no relief, until at length, when they are driven to extremity, they make a desperate effort, roll the burden off upon the Lord Jesus Christ, and exercise a child-like confidence in him. Then they feel relieved; then they feel as if the soul they were praying for would be saved. The burden is gone, and God seems in kindness to sooth down the mind to feel a sweet assurance that the blessing will be granted. Often, after a Christian has had this struggle, this agony in prayer, and has obtained relief in this way, you will find the sweetest and most heavenly affections flow out--the soul rests sweetly and gloriously in God, and rejoices, "with joy unspeakable and full of glory."

Do any of you think now, that there are no such things in the experience of believers? I tell you, if I had time, I could show you from President Edwards, and other approved writers, cases and descriptions just like this. Do you ask why we never have such things here in New York? I tell you, it is not at all because you are so much wiser than Christians are in the country, or because you have so much more intelligence or more enlarged views of the nature of religion, or a more stable and well regulated piety. I tell you, no; instead of priding yourselves in being free from such extravagances, you ought to hide your heads, because Christians in New York are so worldly, and have so much starch, and pride, and fashion, that they cannot come down to such spirituality as this. I wish it could be so. Oh that there might be such a spirit in this city, and in this church! I know it would make a noise, if we had such things done here. But I would not care for that. Let them say, if they please, that the folks in Chatham Chapel are getting deranged. We need not be afraid of that, if we could live near enough to God to enjoy his Spirit in the manner I have described.

These effects of the Spirit of prayer upon the body are themselves no part of religion. It is only that the body is often so weak that the feelings of the soul overpower it. These bodily effects are not at all essential to prevailing prayer, but only a natural or physical result of highly excited emotions of the mind. It is not at all unusual for the body to be weakened and even overcome by any powerful emotion of the mind, on other subjects besides religion. The doorkeeper of Congress in the time of the revolution, fell down dead on the reception of some highly cheering intelligence. I knew a woman in Rochester, who was in a great agony of prayer for the conversion of her son-in-law. One morning he was at an anxious meeting, and she remained at home praying for him. At the close of the meeting, he came home a convert, and she was so rejoiced that she fell down and died on the spot. It is no more strange that these effects should be produced by religion than by strong feeling on any other subject. It is not essential to prayer, but the natural result of great effort of the mind.

Doubtless one great reason why God requires the exercise of this agonizing prayer is, that *it forms such a bond of union between Christ and the Church*. It creates such a sympathy between them. It is as if Christ came and poured the overflowings of his own benevolent heart into his church, and led them to sympathize and to co-operate with him, as they never do in any other way. They feel just as Christ feels--so full of compassion for sinners that they cannot contain themselves. Thus it is often with those ministers who are distinguished for their success in preaching to sinners; they often have such compassion, such overflowing desires for their salvation, that it shows itself in their speaking, and their preaching, just as though Jesus Christ spoke through them. The words come from their lips fresh and warm, as if from the very heart of Christ. I do not mean that he dictates their words; but he excites the feelings that give utterance to them. Then you see a movement in the hearers, as if Christ himself spoke through lips of clay.

This travailing in birth for souls *creates also a remarkable bond of union between warm-hearted Christians and the young converts.* Those who are converted appear very dear to the hearts that have had this spirit of prayer for them. The feeling is like that of a mother for her first-born. Paul expresses it beautifully, when he says, "My little children!" His heart was warm and tender to them. "My little children, of whom I travail in birth again." They had backslidden, and he has all the agonies of a parent over a wandering child. "I travail in birth again, till Christ be formed in you, the hope of glory." In a revival, I have often noticed how those who have had the spirit of prayer, love the young converts. I know this is all algebra to those who have never felt it. But to those who have experienced the agony of wrestling, prevailing prayer, for the conversion of a soul, you may depend upon it, that soul, after it is converted, appears as dear as a child is to the mother who has brought it forth with pain. He has agonized for it, and received it in answer to prayer, and can present it before the Lord Jesus Christ, saying, "Here, Lord, am I, and the children thou hast given me."

Another reason why God requires this sort of prayer is, that *it is the only way in which the church can be properly prepared to receive great blessings without being injured by them.* When the church is thus prostrated in the dust before God, and is in the depth of agony in prayer, the blessing does them good. While at the same time, if they had received the blessing without this deep prostration of soul, it would have puffed them up with pride. But as it is, it increases their holiness, their love, their humility.

Cases of Prevailing Prayer

Elijah the prophet mourned over the declensions of the house of Israel, and when he saw that no other means were likely to be effectual, to prevent a perpetual going away into idolatry, he prayed that the judgments of God might come upon the guilty nation. He prayed that it might not rain, and God shut up the heavens for three years and six months, till the people were driven to the last extremity. And when he saw that it was time to relent, what does he do? See him go up to the mountain and bow down in prayer. He wished to be alone; and he told his servant to go seven times, while he was agonizing in prayer. The last time, the servant told him there was a little cloud appeared, like a man's hand, and he instantly arose from his knees – the blessing was obtained. The time had come for the calamity to be turned back. "Ah, but," you say, "Elijah was a prophet." Now do not make this objection. They made it in the apostle's days, and what does the apostle say? Why he brought forward this very instance, and the fact that Elijah was a man of like passions with ourselves, as a case of prevailing prayer, and insisted that they should pray so too.

John Knox was a man famous for his power in prayer, so that bloody Queen Mary used to say she feared his prayers more than all the armies of Europe. And events showed that she had reason to do it. He used to be in such an agony for the deliverance of his country that he could not sleep. He had a place in his garden where he used to go to pray. One night he and several friends were praying together, and as they prayed, Knox spoke and said that deliverance had come. He could not tell what had happened, but he felt that something had taken place, for God had heard their prayers. What was it? Why the next news they had was, that Mary was dead!

Take a fact which was related, in my hearing, by a minister. He said, that in a certain town there had been no revival for many years; the church was nearly run out, the youth were all unconverted, and desolation reigned unbroken. There lived in a retired part of the town, an aged man, a blacksmith by trade, and of so stammering a tongue, that it was painful to hear him speak. On one Friday, as he was at work in his shop, alone, his mind became greatly exercised about the state of the church, and of the impenitent. His agony became so great, that he was induced to lay by his work, lock the shop door, and spend the afternoon in prayer.

He prevailed, and on the Sabbath called on the minister, and desired him to appoint a conference meeting. After some hesitation, the minister consented, observing, however, that he feared but few would attend. He appointed it the same evening, at a large private house. When evening came, more assembled than could be accommodated in the house. All was silent for a time, until one sinner broke out in tears, and said, if anyone could pray, he begged him to pray for him. Another followed, and another, and still another, until it was found that persons from every quarter of the town were under deep conviction. And what was remarkable was, that they all dated their conviction at the hour when the old man was praying in his shop. A powerful revival followed. Thus this old stammering man prevailed, and, as a prince, had power with God. I could name multitudes of similar cases, but, for want of time, must conclude with a few.

Do Not Quit Before You Have Prevailed

A great deal of prayer is lost, and many people never prevail in prayer, because, when they have desires for particular blessings, they do not follow them up. They may have had desires, benevolent and pure, which were excited by the Spirit of God; and when they have them, they should persevere in prayer, for if they turn off their attention to other objects, they will quench the

Spirit. We tell sinners not to turn off their minds from the one object, but to keep their attention fixed there, till they are saved.

When you find these holy desires in your minds, take care of two things: (1) Do not quench the Spirit, and (2) do not be diverted to other objects. Follow the leadings of the Spirit, till you have offered that effectual fervent prayer that availeth much.

Without the spirit of prayer, ministers will do but little good. A minister need not expect much success, unless he prays for it. Sometimes others may have the spirit of prayer, and obtain a blessing on his labors. Generally, however, those preachers are the most successful who have the most of a spirit of prayer themselves.

Not only must ministers have the spirit of prayer, but it is necessary that the church should unite in offering that effectual fervent prayer which can prevail with God. You need not expect a blessing, unless you ask for it. "For all these things will I be inquired of by the house of Israel, to do it."

Now, my brethren, I have only to ask you, in regard to what I have preached to-night, "Will you do it?" Have you done what I preached to you last Friday evening? Have you gone over with your sins, and confessed them, and got them all out of the way? Can you pray now? And will you join and offer prevailing prayer, that the Spirit of God may come down here?

Questions:

1. How does this chapter challenge your idea of prayer?

2. Describe a time you have heard someone pray with confidence and God answered.

3. What is one thing that you are praying for right now that God has shown you is His will?

Action:

Pray for that item that you just mentioned.

chapter five
The Prayer of Faith

*"I tell you, you can pray for anything,
and if you believe that you've received it,
it will be yours."*

MARK 11:24

These words have been by some supposed to refer exclusively to the faith of miracles. But there is not the least evidence of this. That the text was not designed by our Saviour to refer exclusively to the faith of miracles, is proved by the connection in which it stands. If you read the chapter, you will see that Christ and his apostles were at this time very much engaged in their work, and very prayerful; and as they returned from their places of retirement in the morning, faint and hungry, they saw a fig tree at a little distance. It looked very beautiful, and doubtless gave signs of having fruit on it; but when they came nigh, they found nothing on it but leaves. And Jesus said, "May no one ever eat your fruit again!"

> The next morning as they passed by the fig tree he had cursed, the disciples noticed it had withered from the roots up. Peter remembered what Jesus had said to the tree on the previous day and exclaimed, "Look, Rabbi! The fig tree you cursed has withered and died!"
>
> Then Jesus said to the disciples, "Have faith in God. I tell you the truth, you can say to this mountain, 'May you be lifted up and thrown into the sea,' and it will happen. But you must really believe it will happen and have no doubt in your heart." (Mark 11:20-23 NLT)

Then follow the words of the text: "Therefore I say unto you, What things soever ye desire when ye pray, believe that ye receive them, and ye shall have them."

Our Saviour was desirous of giving his disciples instructions respecting the nature and power of prayer, and the necessity of strong faith in God. He therefore stated a very strong case, a miracle, one so great as the removal of a mountain into the sea. And he tells them, that if they exercise a proper faith in God, they might do such things. But his remarks are not to be limited to faith merely in regard to working miracles, for he goes on to say,

> "But when you are praying, first forgive anyone you are holding a grudge against, so that your Father in heaven will forgive your sins, too." (Mark 11:25 NLT)

Does that relate to miracles? When you pray, you must forgive. Is that required only when a man wishes to work a miracle? There are many other promises in the Bible nearly related to this, and speaking nearly the same language, which have been all disposed of in this short-handed way, as referring to the faith employed in miracles. Just as if the faith of miracles was something different from faith in God!

In my last lecture, I dwelt upon the subject of "prevailing prayer;" and you will recollect that I passed over the subject of faith in prayer very briefly, because I wished to reserve it for a separate discussion. The subject tonight is the prayer of faith. I propose to show that faith is an indispensable condition of prevailing prayer, show what it is that we are to believe when we pray, show when we are bound to exercise this faith, or to believe that we shall receive the thing that we ask for, that this kind of faith in prayer always does obtain the blessing sought, to explain how we are to come into the state of mind in which we can exercise such faith, and to answer several objections which are sometimes alleged against these views of prayer.

Faith is Indispensable to Prayer

That faith is an indispensable condition of prevailing prayer, will not be seriously doubted. There is such a thing as offering benevolent desires, which are acceptable to God as such, that do not include the exercise of faith in regard to the actual reception of those blessings. But such desires are not prevailing prayer, the prayer of faith. God may see fit to grant the things desired, as an act of kindness and love, but it would not be properly in answer to prayer. I am speaking now of the kind of faith that insures the blessing. Do not understand me as saying that there is nothing in prayer that is acceptable to God, or that even obtains the blessing sometimes, without this kind of faith. But I am speaking of the faith which secures the very blessing it seeks. To prove that faith is indispensable to prevailing prayer, it is only necessary to repeat what the apostle James expressly tells us:

> "If you need wisdom, ask our generous God, and he will give it to you. He will not rebuke you for asking. But when you ask him, be sure that your faith is in God alone. Do not waver, for a person with divided loyalty is as unsettled as a wave of the sea that is blown and tossed by the wind." (James 1:5-6 NLT)

What We Believe When We Pray

We are to inquire what we are to believe when we pray.

We are to believe *in the existence of God* – "Anyone who wants to come to him must believe that God exists", and *in his willingness to answer prayer* – "that he rewards those who sincerely seek him" (Hebrews 11:6 NLT). There are many who believe in the existence of God, and do not believe in the efficacy of prayer. They profess to believe in God, but deny the necessity or influence of prayer.

We are to believe *that we shall receive something*. What? Not something, or anything, as it happens, but some particular thing we ask for. We are not to think that God is such a being, that if we ask a fish, he will give us a serpent, or if we ask bread, he will give us a stone. But he says, "I tell you, you can pray for anything, and if you believe that you've received it, it will be yours." With respect to the faith of miracles, it is plain that they were bound to believe they should receive just what they asked for, that the very thing itself should come to pass. That is what they were to believe. Now what ought men to believe in regard to other blessings? Is it

The Prayer of Faith

a mere loose idea, that if a man prays for a specific blessing, God will by some mysterious sovereignty give something or other to him, or something to somebody else, somewhere? When a man prays for his children's conversion, is he to believe that either his children will be converted, or somebody's else children, and it is altogether uncertain which? All this is utter nonsense, and highly dishonorable to God. No, we are to believe that we shall receive the very things that we ask for.

When Are We Bound to Exercise This Faith?

When are we bound to make this prayer? When are we bound to believe that we shall have the very things we pray for? I answer, when we have evidence of it. Faith must always have evidence. A man cannot believe a thing, unless he sees something which he supposes to be evidence. He is under no obligation to believe, and has no right to believe, a thing will be done, unless he has evidence. It is the height of fanaticism to believe without evidence. The kinds of evidence a man may have are the following:

Suppose that *God has especially promised the thing*. As for instance, God says he is more ready to give his Holy Spirit to them that ask him, than parents are to give bread to their children. Here we are bound to believe that we shall receive it when we pray for it. You have no right to put in an "if" and say, "Lord, if it be thy will, give us thy Holy Spirit." This is to insult God. To put an "if" into God's promise, where God has put none, is tantamount to charging God with being insincere. It is like saying, "O God, if thou art in earnest in making these promises, grant us the blessing we pray for."

I heard of a case where a young convert was the means of teaching a minister a solemn truth on the subject of prayer. She was from a very wicked family, and went to live with a minister. While there, she was hopefully converted, and appeared well. One day she came to the minister's study, while he was in it – a thing she was not in the habit of doing; and he thought there must be something the matter. So he asked her to sit down, and kindly inquired into the state of her religious feelings; she said, she was distressed at the manner in which the old church members prayed for the Spirit. They would pray for the Holy Spirit to come, and would seem to be very much in earnest, and plead the promises of God, and then say, "O Lord, if it be thy will, grant us these blessings for Christ's sake." She thought that saying, "if it be thy will," when God has expressly promised it, was questioning whether God was sincere in his promises. The minister tried to reason her out of it, and of course he succeeded in confounding her. But she was distressed and filled with grief, and said, "I cannot argue the point with you, sir, but it is impressed on my mind that it is wrong, and dishonoring God." And she went away weeping with anguish. The minister saw she was not satisfied, and it led him to look at the matter again, and finally he saw that it was putting in an if where God had put none, and where he had revealed his will expressly, and that it was an insult to God. And he went and told his church they were bound to believe that God was in earnest when he made them a promise. And the spirit of prayer came down upon that church, and a most powerful revival followed.

Where there is a general promise in the Scriptures which you may reasonably apply to the particular case before you. If its real meaning includes the particular thing for which you pray, or if you can reasonably apply the principle of the promise to the case, there you have evidence. For instance, suppose it is a time when wickedness prevails greatly, and you are led to pray for God's interference? What promise have you? Why, this one?

"When the enemy shall come in like a flood, the Spirit of the Lord shall lift up a standard against him." Here you see is a general promise laying down a principle of God's administration, which you may apply to the case before you, as a warrant for exercising faith in prayer. And if the case come up, to inquire as to the time in which God will grant blessings in answer to prayer, you have this promise: "While they are yet speaking, I will hear."

There is a vast amount of general promises and principles laid down in the Bible, which Christians might make use of, if they would only think. Whenever you are in circumstances to which the promises or principles apply, there you are to use them. A parent finds this promise: "The mercy of the Lord is from everlasting to everlasting upon them that fear him, and his righteousness unto children's children, to such as keep his covenant, and to those that remember his commandments to do them." Now, here is a promise made to those that possess a certain character. If any parent is conscious that this is his character, he has a rightful ground to apply it to himself and his family. If you have this character, you are bound to make use of this promise in prayer, and believe it, even to your children's children.

If I had time tonight, I could go from one end of the Bible to the other, and produce an astonishing variety of texts that are applicable as promises; enough to prove, that in whatever circumstances a child of God may be placed, God has provided in the Bible some promise, either general or particular, which he can apply, that is precisely suited to his case. Many of God's promises are very broad on purpose to cover much ground. What can be broader than the promise in the text: "I tell you, you can pray for anything?" What praying Christian is there who has not been surprised at the length, and breadth, and fullness, of the promises of God, when the Spirit has applied them to his heart? Who that lives a life of prayer, has not wondered at his own blindness, in not having before seen and felt the extent of meaning and richness of those promises, when viewed under the light of the Spirit of God? At such times he has been astonished at his own ignorance, and found the Spirit applying the promises and declarations of the Bible in a sense in which he had never dreamed of their being applicable before. The manner in which the apostles applied the promises, and prophecies, and declarations of the Old Testament, places in a strong light the breadth of meaning, and fullness, and richness of the word of God. He that walks in the light of God's countenance, and is filled with the Spirit of God as he ought to be, will often make an appropriation of promises to himself, and an application of them to his own circumstances, and the circumstances of those for whom he prays, that a blind professor of religion would never dream of.

Where there is any prophetic declaration, that the thing prayed for is agreeable to the will of God. When it is plain from prophecy that the event is certainly to come, you are bound to believe it, and to make it the ground for your special faith in prayer. If the time is not specified in the Bible, and there is no evidence from other sources, you are not bound to believe that it shall take place now, or immediately. But if the time is specified, or if the time may be learned from the study of the prophecies, and it appears to have arrived, then Christians are under obligations to understand and apply it, by offering the prayer of faith. For instance, take the case of Daniel, in regard to the return of the Jews from captivity. What does he say? "I Daniel understood by books the number of the years whereof the word of the Lord came to Jeremiah the prophet, that he would accomplish seventy years in the desolations of Jerusalem." Here he learned from books, that is, he studied his Bible, and in that way understood that the length of the captivity was to be seventy years. What does he do then? Does he sit down upon the promise, and say, "God has pledged himself to put an end to the captivity in seventy years, and the time has expired, and there is no need of doing anything?" Oh no; he says, "And I set my face unto the Lord God, to seek by prayer and supplications, with fasting, and sackcloth, and ashes." He set himself at once to pray that the thing might be accomplished. He prayed in faith. But what was he to believe? What he had learned from prophecy. There are many prophecies yet unfulfilled, in the Bible, which Christians are bound to understand, as far as they are capable of understanding them, and then make them the basis of believing prayer. Do not think, as some seem to, that because a thing is foretold in prophecy it is not necessary to pray for it, or that it will come whether Christians pray for it or not. There is no truth in this. God says, in regard to this very class of events, which are revealed in prophecy, "Nevertheless, for all these things will I be inquired of by the house of Israel to do it for them."

When the signs of the times, or the providence of God, indicate that a particular blessing is about to be bestowed, we are bound to believe it. The Lord Jesus Christ blamed the Jews, and called them hypocrites, because they did not understand the indications of Providence. They could understand the signs of the weather, and see when it was about to rain, and when it would be fair weather; but they could not see, from the signs of the times, that the time had come for the Messiah to appear, and build up the house of God. There are many professors of religion who are always stumbling and hanging back, whenever anything is proposed to be done. They always say, The time has not come—the time has not come; when there are others who pay attention to the signs of the times, and who have spiritual discernment to understand them. These pray in faith for the blessing, and it comes.

When the Spirit of God is upon you, and excites strong desires for any blessing, you are bound to pray for it in faith. You are bound to infer, from the fact that you find yourself drawn to desire such a thing while in the exercise of such holy affections as the Spirit of God produces, that these desires are the work of the Spirit. People are not apt to desire with the right kind of desires, unless they are excited by the Spirit of God. The apostle refers to these desires, excited by the Spirit, in his epistle to the Romans, where he says:

> And the Holy Spirit helps us in our weakness. For example, we don't know what God wants us to pray for. But the Holy Spirit prays for us with groanings that cannot be expressed in words. And the Father who knows all hearts knows what the Spirit is saying, for the Spirit pleads for us believers in harmony with God's own will. (Romans 8:26-27 NLT)

Here, then, if you find yourself strongly drawn to desire a blessing, you are to understand it as an intimation that God is willing to bestow that particular blessing, and so you are bound to believe it. God does not trifle with his children. He does not go and excite in them a desire for one blessing, to turn them off with something else. But he excites the very desires he is willing to gratify. And when they feel such desires, they are bound to follow them out till they get the blessing.

This Faith Obtains What is Prayed for

This kind of faith always obtains the object. The text is plain here, to show that you shall receive the very thing prayed for. It does not say, "Believe that ye shall receive, and ye shall either have that or something else equivalent to it."

To prove that this faith obtains the very blessing asked, I observe that *otherwise we could never know whether our prayers were answered*. And we might continue praying and praying, long after the prayer was answered by some other blessing equivalent to the one we ask for.

If we are not bound to expect the very thing we ask for, it must be that the Spirit of God deceives us. Why should he excite us to desire a certain blessing, when he means to grant something else?

What is the meaning of this passage, "If a man ask bread, will he give him a stone?" *Does not our Savior rebuke the idea that prayer may be answered by giving something else?* What encouragement have we to pray for anything in particular, if we are to ask for one thing and receive another? Suppose a Christian should pray for a revival here, he would be answered by a revival in China. Or he might pray for a revival, and God would send the cholera, or an earthquake. All the history of the church shows that when God answers prayer, he gives his people the very thing for which their prayers are offered. God confers other blessings, on both saints and sinners, which they do not pray for at all. He sends his rain both upon the just and the unjust, But when he answers prayer, it is by doing what they ask him to do. To be sure, he often more than answers prayer. He grants them not only what they ask, but often connects other blessings with it.

Perhaps you may feel a difficulty here about the prayers of Jesus Christ. People may often ask, "Did not he pray in the garden for the cup to be removed, and was his prayer answered?" I answer that this is no difficulty at all, for the prayer was answered. The cup he prayed to be delivered from was removed. This is what the apostle refers to, when he says, "While Jesus was here on earth, he offered prayers and pleadings, with a loud cry and tears, to the one who could rescue him from death. And God heard his prayers because of his deep reverence for God" (Hebrews 5:7 NLT). Now I ask, on what occasion was he saved from death, if not on this? Was it the death of the cross he prayed to be delivered from? Not at all. But the case was this. A short time before he was betrayed, we hear him saying to his disciples, "My soul is exceedingly sorrowful, even unto death." Anguish of mind came rolling in upon him, till he was just ready to die, and he went out into the garden to pray, and told his disciples to watch, and then he went by himself and prayed; "My Father! If it is possible, let this cup of suffering be taken away from me. Yet I want your will to be done, not mine" (Matthew 26:39 NLT). In his agony he rose from his knees, and walked the garden, till he came where his disciples were, and there he saw them fast asleep. He awaked them and said, "What, could ye not watch with me one hour?" And then he went again, for he was in such distress that he could not stand still, and again he poured out his soul. And the third time he goes away and prays, "Father, if you are willing, please take this cup of suffering away from me. Yet I want your will to be done, not mine" (Luke 22:42 NLT). And now the third time of praying, there appeared an angel unto him from heaven, strengthening him. And his mind became composed, and calm, and the cup was gone. Till then, he

The Prayer of Faith

had been in such an agony that his sweat was as it were great drops of blood, but now it was all over.

Some have supposed that he was praying against the cross, and begging to be delivered from dying on the cross! Did Christ ever shrink from the cross? Never. He came into the world on purpose to die on the cross, and he never shrunk from it. But he was afraid he should die in the garden before he came to the cross. The burden on his soul was so great, and produced such an agony, that he felt as if he was on the point of dying, His soul was sorrowful even unto death. But after the angel appeared unto him, we hear no more of his agony of soul. He had prayed for relief from that cup, and his prayer was answered. He became calm, and had no more mental suffering till just as he expired. This case, therefore, is no exception. He received the very thing for which he asked, as he says, "You always hear me." (John 11:42 NLT)

But there is another case often brought up, where the apostle Paul prayed against the thorn in the flesh. He says, "Three different times I begged the Lord to take it away." (2 Corinthians 12:8 NLT). And God answered him, "My grace is all you need." (v.9 NLT) It is the opinion of Dr. Clarke and others, that Paul's prayer was answered in the very thing for which he prayed. That "the thorn in the flesh, the messenger of Satan," of which he speaks, was a false apostle who had distracted and perverted the church at Corinth. That Paul prayed against his influence, and the Lord answered him by assuring him, "My grace is all you need." Who does not know that it was, and that Paul's influence ultimately triumphed?

But admitting that Paul's prayer was not answered by granting the particular thing for which he prayed, in order to make out this case as an exception to the prayer of faith, they are obliged to assume the very thing to be proved; and that is, that the apostle prayed in faith. There is no reason to suppose that Paul would always pray in faith, any more than that any other Christian does. The very manner in which God answered him shows that it was not in faith. He virtually tells him, "That thorn is necessary for your sanctification, and to keep you from being exalted above measure. I sent it upon you in love, and in faithfulness, and you have no business to pray that I should take it away. LET IT ALONE."

There is not only no evidence that he prayed in faith, but a strong presumption that he did not. From the history it is evident that he had nothing on which to repose faith. There was no express promise, no general promise, that could be applicable, no providence of God, no prophecy, no teaching of the Spirit that God would remove this thorn; but the presumption was that God would not remove it. He had given it to him for a particular purpose. His prayer appears to have been selfish, or at least praying against a mere personal influence. This was not any personal suffering that retarded his usefulness, but on the contrary it was given him to increase his usefulness by keeping him humble; and because on some account he found it inconvenient and mortifying, he set himself to pray out of his own heart, evidently without being led to it by the Spirit of God. But did Paul pray in faith without the Spirit of God, any more than any other man? And will anyone undertake to say that the Spirit of God led him to pray that this might be removed, when God himself had given it for a particular purpose, which purpose could not be answered only as the thorn continued with him?

Why then is this made an exception to the general rule laid down in the text, that a man shall receive whatsoever he asks in

The Prayer of Faith

faith? I was once amazed and grieved at a public examination at a Theological Seminary, to hear them darken counsel by words without knowledge on this subject. This case of Paul, and that of Christ just adverted to, were both of them cited as instances to prove to their students that the prayer of faith would not be answered in the particular thing for which they prayed. Now to teach such sentiments as these in or out of a Theological Seminary, is to trifle with the word of God, and to break the power of the Christian ministry. Has it come to this, that our grave doctors in our seminaries, are employed to instruct Zion's watchmen, to believe and teach that it is not to be expected that the prayer of faith is to be answered in granting the object for which we pray? Oh, tell it not in Gath, nor let the sound reach Askelon! What is to become of the church while such are the views of its gravest and most influential ministers? I would not be unkind nor censorious, but as one of the ministers of Jesus Christ, I feel bound to bear testimony against such a perversion of the word of God.

It is evident that the prayer of faith will obtain the blessing, from the fact that *our faith rests on evidence that to grant that thing is the will of God*. Not evidence that something else will be granted, but that this particular thing will be. But how, then, can we have evidence that this thing will be granted, if another thing is to be granted? People often receive more than they pray for. Solomon prayed for wisdom, and God granted him riches and honor in addition. So a wife sometimes prays for the conversion of her husband, and if she offers the prayer, of faith, God may not only grant that blessing, but convert her child, and her whole family. Blessings sometimes seem to hang together, so that if a Christian gains one he gets them all.

* * *

How Do Our Minds Offer Such Prayer?

People sometimes ask, "How shall I offer such prayer? Shall I say, Now I will pray in faith for such and such a blessing?" No, the human mind is not moved in this way. You might just as well say, "Now I will call up a spirit from the bottomless pit."

You must first obtain evidence that God will bestow the blessing. How did Daniel make out to offer the prayer of faith? He searched the Scriptures. Now, you need not let your Bible lie on a shelf, and expect God to reveal his promises to you. Search the Scriptures, and see where you can get either a general or special promise, or a prophecy, on which you can plant your feet when you pray. Go through the Bible, and you will find it full of such things, precious promises, which you may plead in faith. You never need to want for objects of prayer, if you will do as Daniel did. Persons are staggered on this subject, because they never make a proper use of the Bible.

A curious case occurred in one of the towns in the western part of this state. There was a revival there. A certain clergyman came to visit the place, and heard a great deal said about the Prayer of Faith. He was staggered at what they said, for he had never regarded the subject in the light they did. He inquired about it of the minister that was laboring there. The minister requested him, in a kind spirit, to go home, and take his Testament, look out the passages that refer to prayer, and go round to his most praying people, and ask them how they understood these passages. He said he would do it, for though these views were new to him, he was willing to learn. He did it, and went to his praying men and women, and read the passages without note or comment, and asked what they thought. He found their plain common sense had

The Prayer of Faith

led them to understand these passages, and to believe that they mean just as they say. This affected him, and then the fact of his going round and presenting the promises before their minds awakened the spirit of prayer in them, and a revival followed.

I could name many individuals who have set themselves to examine the Bible on this subject, and before they got half through with it have been filled with the spirit of prayer. They found that God meant by his promises just what a plain, common sense man would understand them to mean. I advise you to try it. You have Bibles; look them over, and whenever you find a promise that you can use, fasten it in your mind before you go on; and I venture to predict you will not get through the book without finding out that God's promises mean just what they say.

Cherish the good desires you have. Christians very often lose their good desires by not attending to this; and then their prayers are mere words, without any desire or earnestness at all. The least longing of desire must be cherished. If your body was likely to freeze, and you had even the least spark of fire, how you would cherish it! So if you have the least desire for a blessing, let it be ever so small, do not trifle it away. Do not grieve the Spirit. Do not be diverted. Do not lose good desires by levity, by censoriousness, by worldly-mindedness. Watch and pray, and follow it up, or you will never pray the prayer of faith.

Entire consecration to God is indispensable to the prayer of faith. You must live a holy life, and consecrate all to God – your time, talents, influence – all you have, and all you are, to be his entirely. Read the lives of pious men, and you will be struck with this fact: that they used to set apart times to renew their covenant, and dedicate themselves anew to God; and whenever they have done so, a blessing has always followed immediately. If I had Edwards here to-night, I could read passages showing how it was in his days.

You must persevere. You are not to pray for a thing once, and then cease, and call that the prayer of faith. Look at Daniel. He prayed twenty-one days, and did not cease till he had obtained the blessing. He set his heart and his face unto the Lord, to seek by prayer and supplications, with fasting, and sackcloth, and ashes: and he held on three weeks, and then the answer came. And why did not it come before? God sent an Archangel to bear the message, but the devil hindered him all this time. See what Christ says in the parable of the unjust judge, and the parable of the loaves. What does he teach us by them? Why, that God will grant answers to prayer when it is importunate. "Shall not God avenge his own elect, who cry day and night unto him?"

If you would pray in faith, be sure to walk every day with God. If you do, *he will tell you what to pray for.* Be filled with his Spirit, and he will give you objects enough to pray for. He will give you as much of the spirit of prayer as you have strength of body to bear.

Said a good man to me, "Oh, I am dying for the want of strength to pray. My body is crushed, the world is on me, and how can I forbear praying!" I have known that man go to bed absolutely sick, for weakness and faintness, under the pressure. And I have known him pray as if he would do violence to heaven, and then seen the blessing come as plainly in answer to his prayer as if it was revealed, so that no person would doubt it any more than if God had spoken from heaven. Shall I tell you how he died? He prayed more and more, and he used to take the map of the world before him and pray, and look over the different countries and pray for them, till he absolutely expired in his room praying. Blessed man!

He was the reproach of the ungodly and of carnal, unbelieving professors, but he was the favorite of heaven, and a prevailing prince in prayer.

Addressing Objections to the Prayer of Faith

I will refer to some objections which are brought forward against this doctrine.

"*It leads to fanaticism and amounts to a new revelation.*" Why should this be a stumbling block? They must have evidence to believe before they can offer the prayer of faith. And if God gives other evidence besides the senses, where is the objection? True, there is a sense in which this is a new revelation; it is making known a thing by his Spirit. But it is the very revelation which God has promised to give. It is just the one we are to expect, if the Bible is true; that when we know not what we ought to pray for, according to the will of God, his Spirit helps our infirmities, and teaches us the very thing to pray for. Shall we deny the teaching of the Spirit?

It is often asked, "*Is it our duty to pray the prayer of faith for the salvation of all men?*" I answer, No; for that is not a thing according to the will of God. It is directly contrary to his revealed will. We have no evidence that all will be saved. We should feel benevolently to all, and, in itself considered, desire their salvation. But God has revealed it to us that many of the human race shall be damned. And it cannot be a duty to believe that they shall all be saved, in the face of a revelation to the contrary. In Christ's prayer, in the seventeenth chapter of John, he expressly said, "I pray not for the world but for those thou hast given me."

But say some, "If we were to offer this prayer for all men, *would not all men be saved?*" I answer, Yes, and so they would be saved, if they would all repent. But they will not. Neither will Christians offer the prayer of faith for all, because there is no evidence on which to ground a belief that God intends to save all men.

But you ask, "*For whom are we to offer this prayer?* We want to know in what cases, for what persons, and places, and at what times, etc., we are to make the prayer of faith." I answer, as I have already answered, When you have evidence, from promises, or prophecies, or providences, or the leadings of the Spirit, that God will do the things you pray for.

"*How is it that so many prayers of pious parents for their children are not answered?* Did you not say there was a promise which pious parents may apply to their children? Why is it, then, that so many pious praying parents have had impenitent children, that died in their sins?" Granted that it is so, what does it prove? Let God be true, but every man a liar. Which shall we believe, that God's promise has failed, or that these parents did not do their duty? Perhaps they did not believe the promise, or did not believe there was any such thing as the prayer of faith. Wherever you find a professor that does not believe in any such prayer, you find, as a general thing, that he has children and domestics yet in their sins. And no wonder, unless they are converted in answer to the prayers of somebody else.

"*Will not these views lead to fanaticism?* Will not many people think they are offering the prayer of faith when they are not?" That is the same objection that the Unitarians make against the doctrine of regeneration – that many people think they have been born again when they have not. It is an argument against all spiritual religion whatever. Some think they have it when they have not,

The Prayer of Faith

and are fanatics. But there are those who know what the prayer of faith is, just as there are those who know what spiritual experience is, though it may stumble cold-hearted professors who know it not. Even ministers often lay themselves open to the rebuke which Christ gave to Nicodemus: "You are a respected Jewish teacher, and yet you don't understand these things?" (John 3:10 NLT).

Do Not Restrain the Prayer of Faith

Persons who have not known by experience what this is, have great reason to doubt their piety. This is by no means uncharitable. Let them examine themselves. It is to be feared that they understand prayer as Nicodemus did the new birth. They have not walked with God, and you cannot describe it to them, any more than you can describe a beautiful painting to a blind man who cannot see colors. Many professors can understand about the prayer of faith just as much as a blind man does of colors.

There is reason to believe millions are in hell because professors have not offered the prayer of faith. When they had promises under their eye, they have not had faith enough to use them. Thus parents let their children, and even baptized children, go down to hell because they would not believe the promises of God. Doubtless many women's husbands have gone to hell, when they might have prevailed with God in prayer and saved them. The signs of the times and the indications of Providence were favorable, perhaps, and the Spirit of God prompted desires for their salvation, and they had evidence enough to believe that God was ready to grant a blessing, and if they had only prayed in faith,

God would have granted it; but God turned it away because they would not discern the signs of the times.

You say, "This leaves the church under a great load of guilt." True, it does so; and no doubt multitudes will stand up before God covered all over with the blood of souls that have been lost through their want of faith. The promises of God, accumulated in their Bibles, will stare them in the face and weigh them down to hell.

Many professors of religion live so far from God that to talk to them about the prayer of faith is all unintelligible. Very often the greatest offence possible to them is to preach about this kind of prayer.

* * *

I want to ask the professors who are here a few questions. Do you know what it is to pray in faith? Did you ever pray in this way? Have you ever prayed till your mind was assured the blessing would come – till you felt that rest in God, that confidence, as perfect as if you saw God come down from heaven to give it to you? If not, you ought to examine your foundation. How can you live without praying in faith at all? How do you live in view of your children, while you have no assurance whatever that they will be converted? One would think you would go deranged. I knew a father at the West; he was a good man, but he had erroneous views respecting the prayer of faith; and his whole family of children were grown up and not one of them converted. At length his son sickened and seemed about to die. The father prayed, but the son grew worse and seemed sinking into the grave without hope. The father prayed till his anguish was unutterable. He went at last and

The Prayer of Faith

prayed — (there seemed no prospect of his son's life) — but he poured out his soul as if he would not be denied, till at length he got an assurance that his son would not only live, but be converted; and not only this one, but his whole family, would be converted to God. He came into the house and told his family his son would not die. They were astonished at him. "I tell you," says he, "he won't die. And no child of mine will ever die in his sins." That man's children were all converted years ago.

What do you think of that? Was that fanaticism? If you believe so, it is because you know nothing about the matter. Do you pray so? Do you live in such a manner that you can offer such prayer for your children? I know that the children of professors may sometimes be converted in answer to the prayers of somebody else. But ought you to live so? Dare you trust to the prayers of others when God calls you to sustain this most important relation to your children?

Finally, see what combined effort is made to dispose of the Bible. The wicked are for throwing away the threatenings of the Bible, and the church the promises. And what is there left? Between them, they leave the Bible a blank. I say it in love: What are our Bibles good for if we do not lay hold on their precious promises, and use them as the ground of our faith when we pray for the blessing of God? You had better send your Bibles to the heathen, where they will do some good, if you are not going to believe and use them. I have no evidence that there is much of this prayer now in this church or in this city. And what will become of it? What will become of your children? Your neighbors? The wicked?

* * *

Questions:

1. Where did this chapter challenge your thinking on prayer?

2. What is an example from the Bible where someone prayed the prayer of faith?

3. Can you think of an example when you prayed like this and God answered?

4. What is an example of something that God has promised to your heart that you can pray?

Action:

Take some time to pray the prayer of faith on an item the Holy Spirit has put on your heart.

chapter six
Meetings for Prayer

"I also tell you this: If two of you agree here on earth concerning anything you ask, my Father in heaven will do it for you."

MATTHEW 18: 19 (NLT)

Hitherto, in treating of the subject of Prayer, I have confined my remarks to secret prayer. I am now to speak of social prayer, or prayer offered in company, where two or more are united in praying. Such meetings have been common from the time of Christ, and even hundreds of years before. And it is probable that God's people have always been in the habit of making united supplication, whenever they had the privilege. The propriety of the practice will not be questioned here. I need not dwell now on the duty of social prayer. Nor is it my design to discuss the question, whether any two Christians agreeing to ask any blessing, will be sure to obtain it. My object is to make some remarks on meetings for prayer, discussing the design of Prayer Meetings, the manner of conducting them, and to mention several things that will defeat the design of holding them.

The Design of Prayer Meetings

One design of assembling several persons together for united prayer, is *to promote union among Christians*. Nothing tends more to cement the hearts of Christians than praying together. Never do they love one another so well as when they witness the outpouring of each other's hearts in prayer. Their spirituality begets a feeling of union and confidence, highly important to the prosperity of the church. It is doubtful whether Christians can ever be otherwise than united, if they are in the habit of really praying together. And where they have had hard feelings and differences among themselves, they are all done away, by uniting in prayer. The great object is gained, if you can bring them really to unite in prayer. If this can be done, the difficulties vanish.

To extend the spirit of prayer. God has so constituted us, and such is the economy of his grace, that we are sympathetic beings, and communicate our feelings to each other. A minister, for instance, will often as it were breathe his own feelings into his congregation. The Spirit of God that inspires his soul, makes use of his feelings to influence his hearers, just as much as he makes use of the words he preaches. So he makes use of the feelings of Christians. Nothing is more calculated to beget a spirit of prayer, than to unite in social prayer, with one who has the spirit himself; unless this one should be so far ahead that his prayer will repel the rest. His prayer will awaken them, if they are not so far behind as to revolt at it and resist it. If they are anywhere near the standard of his feelings, his spirit will kindle, and burn, and spread all around. One individual in a church, that obtains a spirit of prayer, will often arouse a whole church, and extend the same spirit through the whole, and a general revival follows.

Another grand design of social prayer, is *to move God*. Not that it changes the mind and feelings of God. When we speak of moving God, as I have said in a former lecture, we do not mean that it alters the will of God. But when the right kind of prayer is offered by Christians, they are in such a state of mind, that it becomes proper for God to bestow a blessing. They are then prepared to receive it, and he gives because he is always the same, and always ready and happy to show mercy. When Christians are united, and praying as they ought, God opens the windows of heaven, and pours out his blessings till there is not room to receive them.

Another important design of prayer meetings is *the conviction and conversion of sinners*. When properly conducted, they are eminently calculated to produce this effect. Sinners are apt to be solemn when they hear Christians pray. Where there is a spirit of prayer, sinners must feel. An ungodly man, a Universalist, once said respecting a certain minister, "I can bear his preaching very well, but when he prays, I feel awfully; I feel as if God was coming down upon me." Sinners are often convicted by hearing prayer. A young man of distinguished talents, known to many of you, said concerning a certain minister to whom before his conversion he had been very much opposed, "As soon as he began to pray, I began to be convicted, and if he had continued to pray much longer, I should not have been able to contain myself." Just as soon as Christians begin to pray as they ought, sinners then know that they pray, and they feel awfully. They do not understand what spirituality is, because they have no experience of it. But when such prayer is offered, they know there is something in it; they know God is in it, and it brings them near to God; it makes them feel awfully solemn, and they cannot bear it. And not only is it calculated to impress the minds of sinners, but when Christians pray in faith, the Spirit of God is poured out, and sinners are melted down and converted on the spot.

The Manner of Conducting Prayer Meetings

It is often well to *open a prayer meeting by reading a short portion of the word of God*; especially if the person who takes the lead of the meeting, can call to mind any portion that will be applicable to the object or occasion, and that is impressive, and to the point. If he has no passage that is applicable, he had better not read any at all. Do not drag in the word of God to make up part of the meeting as a mere matter of form. This is an insult to God. It is not well to read any more than is applicable to the subject before the meeting, or the occasion. Some people think it always necessary to read a whole chapter, though it may be ever so long, and have a variety of subjects.

It is just as impressive and judicious to read a whole chapter, as it would be for a minister to take a whole chapter for his text, when his object was to make some particular truth bear on the minds of his audience. The design of a prayer meeting should be to bring Christians to the point to pray for a definite object. Wandering over a large field, hinders and destroys this design.

It is proper that *the person who leads should make some short and appropriate remarks*, calculated to explain the nature of prayer, and the encouragements we have to pray, and to bring the object to be prayed for directly before the minds of the people.

Meetings for Prayer

A man can no more pray without having his thoughts concentrated, than he can do anything else. The person leading, should therefore see to this, by bringing up before their minds the object they came to pray for. If they came to pray for any object he can do this. And if they did not, they had better go home. It is of no use to stay there and mock God, by pretending to pray, when they have nothing on earth to pray for.

After stating the object, he should bring up some promise or some principle, as the ground of encouragement to expect an answer to their prayers. If there is any indication of Providence, or any promise, or any principle in the Divine government that affords a ground of faith, let him call it to mind, and not let them be talking out of their own hearts at random, without knowing any solid reason to expect an answer. One reason why prayer meetings mostly accomplish so little, is because there is so little common sense exercised about them. Instead of looking round for some solid footing on which to repose their faith, they just come together and pour forth their words, and neither know nor care whether they have any reason to expect an answer. If they are going to pray about anything concerning which there can be any doubt or any mistake, in regard to the ground of faith, they should be shown the reason there is for believing that their prayers will be heard and answered. It is easy to see, that unless something like this is done, three-fourths of them will have no idea of what they are doing, or of the ground on which they should expect to receive what they pray for.

In calling on persons to pray, it is always desirable to *let things take their own course wherever it is safe*. If it can be left so with safety, let those pray who are most inclined to pray. It sometimes happens that even those who are ordinarily the most spiritual, and most proper to be called on, are not at the time in a suitable frame; they may be cold and worldly, and only freeze the meeting. But if you let those pray who desire to pray, you avoid this. But often this cannot be done with safety, especially in large cities, where a prayer meeting might be liable to be interrupted by those who have no business to pray; some fanatic or crazy person, some hypocrite or enemy, who would only make a noise. In most places, however, this course may be taken with perfect safety. Give up the meeting to the Spirit of God, Those who desire to pray, let them pray. If the leader sees anything that needs to be set right, let him remark, freely and kindly, and put it right, and then go on again. Only, he should be careful to time his remarks, so as not to interrupt the flow of feeling, or to chill the meeting, or turn off the minds from the proper subject.

If it is necessary to name the individuals who are to pray, it is best to *call on those who are most spiritual first.* And if you do not know who they are, then those whom you would naturally suppose to be most alive. If they pray at the outset, they will be likely to spread the spirit of prayer through the meeting, and elevate the tone of the whole. Otherwise, if you call on those who are cold and lifeless at the beginning, they will be likely to diffuse a chill throughout the meeting. The only hope of having an efficient prayer meeting is when at least a part of the church is spiritual, and they infuse their spirit into the rest. This is the very reason why it is often best to let things take their course, for then those who have the most feeling are apt to pray first, and give character to the meeting.

The prayers should always be very short. When individuals suffer themselves to pray long, they forget where they are, that they are only the mouth of the congregation, and that the congregation cannot be expected to sympathize with them, so as to go along and feel united in prayer, if they are long and tedious, and go all around the world and pray for everything that they can think of. Commonly, those who pray long in meeting, do it not because they have the spirit of prayer, but because they have not. And they go round and round, not because they are full of prayer. Some men will spin out a long prayer in telling God who and what he is, or they exhort God to do so and so. Some pray out a whole system of divinity. Some preach, some exhort the people, till everybody wishes they would stop, and God wishes so too, undoubtedly. They should keep to the point, and pray for what they came to pray for, and not follow the imagination of their own foolish hearts all over the universe.

Each one should pray for some one object. It is well for every individual to have one object for prayer: two or more may pray for the same thing, or each a separate object. If the meeting is convened to pray for some specific thing, let them all pray for that. If its object is more general, let them select their subjects, according as they feel interested in them. If one feels particularly disposed to pray for the church, let him do it. If the next feels disposed to pray for the church, he may do so too. Perhaps the next will feel inclined to pray for sinners; for the youth; to confess sin; let him do it, and as soon as he has got through let him stop. Whenever a man has deep feeling, he always feels on some particular point, and if he prays for that, he will speak out of the abundance of his heart, and then he will naturally stop when he is done. Those who feel most, will be most ready to confine their prayers to that point, and stop when they have done and not pray all over the world.

If in the progress of the meeting it becomes necessary to change the object of prayer, let the man who leads state the fact, and explain it in a few words. If the object is to pray for the church, or for backsliders, or sinners, or the heathen, let him state it plainly, and then turn it over and hold it up before them till he brings them to think and feel deeply before they pray. Then state to them the grounds on which they may repose their faith in regard to obtaining the blessings they pray for, if any such statement is needed, and so lead them right up to the throne, and let them take hold of the hand of God. This is according to the philosophy of the mind. People always do it for themselves when they pray in secret, if they really mean to pray to any purpose. And so it should be in prayer meetings.

It is important that *the time should be fully occupied, so as not to leave long seasons of silence.* This always makes a bad impression and chills the meeting. I know that sometimes churches have seasons of silent prayer. But in those cases they should be specially requested to pray in silence, so that all may know why they are silent. This often has a most powerful effect, where a few moments are spent by a whole congregation in silence, while all lift up their thoughts to God. This is very different from having long intervals of silence because there is nobody to pray. Everyone feels that such a silence is like the cold damp of death over the meeting.

It is exceedingly important that *he who leads the meeting should press sinners who may be present to immediate repentance.* He should crowd this hard, and urge the Christians present to pray in such a way as to make sinners feel that they are expected to repent immediately. This tends to inspire Christians with compassion and love for souls. The remarks made to sinners are often like pouring fire upon the hearts of Christians, to awaken them to prayer and effort for their conversion. Let them see and feel the guilt and danger of sinners right among them, and then they will pray.

Those Things which Defeat a Prayer Meeting

I am to mention several things which may defeat the design of a prayer meeting.

When there is an unhappy want of confidence in the leader, there is no hope of any good. Whatever the cause may be, whether he is to blame or not, the very fact that he leads the meeting will cast a damp over it and prevent all good. I have witnessed it in churches, where there was some offensive elder or deacon, perhaps justly offensive, and perhaps not, set to lead the prayer meeting, and the meeting would all die under his influence. If there is a want of confidence in regard to his piety, or in his ability, or in his judgment, or in anything connected with the meeting, everything he says or does will fall to the ground. The same thing often takes place where the church has lost their confidence in the minister.

Where the leader lacks spirituality, there will be a dryness and coldness in his remarks and prayers, and everything will indicate his want of unction, and his whole influence will be the very reverse of what it ought to be. I have known churches where a prayer meeting could not be sustained, and the reason was not obvious, but those who understood the state of things knew that the leader was so notorious for his want of spirituality, that he would inevitably freeze a prayer meeting to death. In many Presbyterian churches the elders are so far from being spiritual men that they always freeze a prayer meeting. And then they are often amazingly jealous for their dignity, and cannot bear to have anybody else lead the meeting. And if any member that is spiritual takes the lead of a prayer meeting, they will take him to task for it: "Why, you are not an elder, and ought not to lead a prayer meeting in presence of an elder." And thus they stand in the way, while the whole church is suffering under their blighting influence.

A man who knows he is not in a spiritual frame of mind has no business to conduct a prayer meeting; he will kill it. There are two reasons: First, he will have no spiritual discernment, and will not know what to do, or when to do it. A person who is spiritual can see the movements of Providence, and can feel the Spirit of God, and understand what he is leading them to pray for, so as to time his subjects, and take advantage of the state of feeling among Christians. He will not overthrow all the feeling in a meeting by introducing other things that are incongruous or ill-timed. He has spiritual discernment to understand the leadings of the Spirit, and his workings in those who pray, and to follow on as the Spirit leads. Suppose an individual leads who is not spiritual, and there are two or three prayers, and the spirit of prayer rises, but the leader has no spiritual discernment to see it, and he makes some remarks on another point, or reads a piece out of some book, that is as far from the feeling of the meeting as the north pole. It may be just as evident to others what they are called to pray for, as if the Son of God himself had come into the meeting and named the subject; but the leader will overthrow it all, because he is so stupid that he does not know the indications of the meeting.

And then, if the leader is not spiritual, he will very likely be dull and dry in his remarks and in all his exercises. He will read a long hymn in a dreamy manner, and then read a long passage of Scripture, in a tone so cold and wintry that he will spread a wintry pall over the meeting, and it will be dull as long as his cold heart is placed up in front of the whole thing.

Meetings for Prayer

A want of suitable talents in the leader. If he is wanting in that kind of talents which are fitted to make a meeting useful, he will injure the meeting. If he can say nothing, or if his remarks are so out of the way as to produce levity or contempt, or if they have nothing in them that will impress the mind, or are not guided by good sense, or not appropriate, he will injure the meeting. A man may be pious, but so weak that his prayers do not edify, but rather disgust, the people present. When this is so, he had better keep silence.

Sometimes the benefit of a prayer-meeting is defeated by *a bad spirit in the leader.* For instance when there is a revival, and great opposition, if a leader gets up in a prayer meeting and speaks of instances of opposition, and comments upon them, and thus diverts the meeting away from the object they come to pray for, he knows not what spirit he is of. Its effect is always ruinous to a prayer meeting. Let a minister in a revival come out and preach against the opposition, and he will infallibly destroy the revival, and turn the hearts of Christians away from their proper object. Let the man who is set to lead the church be careful to guard his own spirit, lest he should mislead the church, and diffuse a wrong temper. The same will be true, if any one who is called upon to speak or pray, introduces in his remarks or prayers anything controversial, impertinent, unreasonable, unscriptural, ridiculous or irrelevant. Any of these things will quench the tender breathings of the spirit of prayer, and destroy the meeting.

Persons coming late to the meeting. This is a very great hindrance to a prayer meeting. When people have begun to pray, and their attention is fixed, and they have shut their eyes and closed their ears, to keep out everything from their minds, in the midst of a prayer somebody will come bolting in and walk up through the room. Some will look up, and all have their minds interrupted for the moment. Then they all get fixed again, and another comes in, and so on. Why, I suppose the devil would not care how many Christians went to a prayer-meeting, if they will only go after the meeting is begun. He would be glad to have ever so many go scattering along so, and dodging in very piously after the meeting is begun.

When persons make cold prayers, and cold confessions of sin, they are sure to quench the spirit of prayer. When the influences of the Spirit are enjoyed, in the midst of the warm expressions that are flowing forth, let an individual come in who is cold, and pour his cold breath out, like the damp of death, and it will make every Christian that has any feeling want to get out of the meeting.

When the meeting is overly programmed. In some places it is common to begin a prayer meeting by reading a long portion of Scripture. Then the deacon or elder gives out a long hymn. Next, they sing it. Then he prays a long prayer, praying for the Jews and the fullness of the Gentiles, and many other objects that have nothing to do with the occasion of the meeting. After that perhaps he reads a long extract from some book or magazine. Then they have another long hymn and another long prayer, and then they go home. I once heard an elder say, they had kept up a prayer meeting so many years, and yet there had been no revival in the place. The truth was, that the officers of the church had been accustomed to carry on the meetings in just such a dignified way, and their dignity would not allow anything to be altered. No wonder there was no revival. Such prayer meetings are enough to hinder a revival. And if ever so many revivals should commence, the prayer meeting would destroy them. There was a prayer meeting once in this city, as I have been told, where there appeared to be some feeling, and some one proposed that they should have two or three prayers in succession, without rising from their knees. One dignified man present opposed it, and said that they never had done so, and he hoped there would be no innovations. He did not approve of innovations. And that was the last of the revival. Such persons have their prayer meetings stereotyped, and they are determined not to turn out of their track, whether they have the blessing or not. To allow any such thing would be a new measure, and they never like new measures.

A great deal of singing often injures a prayer meeting. The agonizing spirit of prayer does not lead people to sing. There is a time for everything; a time to sing, and a time to pray. But if I know what it is to travail in birth for souls, Christians never feel less like singing, than when they have the spirit of prayer for sinners. Singing is the natural expression of feelings that are joyful and cheerful. The spirit of prayer is not a spirit of joy. It is a spirit of travail, and agony of soul, supplicating and pleading with God with strong cryings, and groanings that cannot be uttered. This is more like anything else than it is like singing. I have known states of feeling, where you could not distress the people of God more than to begin to sing. It would be so entirely different from their feelings. Why, if you knew your house was on fire, would you first stop and sing a hymn before you put it out? How would it look here in New York, when a building was on fire, and the firemen are all collected, for the foreman to stop and sing a hymn? It is just about as natural for the people to sing when exercised with a spirit of prayer. When people feel like pulling men out of the fire, they do not feel like singing. I never knew a singing revival amount to much. Its tendency is to do away all deep feeling. It is true that singing a hymn has sometimes produced a powerful effect upon sinners who are convicted, but in general it is the perfect contrast there is between their feelings and those of the happy souls who sing, that produces the effect. If the hymn be of a joyful character it is not directly calculated to benefit sinners, and is highly fitted to relieve the mental anguish of the Christian, so as to destroy that travail of soul which is indispensable to his prevailing in prayer.

When singing is introduced in a prayer-meeting, the hymns should be short, and so selected as to bring out something solemn; some striking words, such as the Judgment Hymn, and others calculated to produce an effect on sinners; or something that will produce a deep impression on the minds of Christians; but not that joyful kind of singing, that makes everybody feel comfortable, and turns off the mind from the object of the prayer meeting.

I once heard a celebrated organist produce a remarkable effect in a protracted meeting. The organ was a powerful one, and the double bass pipes were like thunder. The hymn was given out that has these lines:

> See the storm of vengeance gathering
> O'er the path you dare to tread;
> "Hear the awful thunder rolling,
> Loud and louder o'er your head."

When he came to these words, we first heard the distant roar of thunder, then it grew nearer and louder, till at the word "louder," there was a crash that seemed almost to overpower the whole congregation.

Such things in their proper place do good. But common singing dissipates feeling. It should always be such as not to take away feeling, but to deepen it.

Often a prayer meeting is injured by calling on the young

converts to sing joyful hymns. This is highly improper in a prayer meeting. It is no time for them to let feeling flow away in joyful singing, while so many sinners around them, and their own former companions, are going down to hell. A revival is often put down by the church and minister all giving themselves up to singing with young converts. Thus by stopping to rejoice, when they ought to feel more and more deeply for sinners, they grieve away the Spirit of God, and they soon find that their agony and travail of soul are all gone.

Introducing *subjects of controversy* into prayer will defeat a prayer meeting. Nothing of a controversial nature should be introduced into prayer, unless it is the object of the meeting to settle that thing. Otherwise, let Christians come together in their prayer-meetings, on the broad ground of offering united prayer for a common object. And let controversies be settled somewhere else.

Great pains should be taken, both by the leader and others, to watch narrowly the motions of the Spirit of God. Let them not pray without the Spirit, but follow his leadings. Be sure not to quench the Spirit for the sake of praying according to the regular custom. Avoid everything calculated to divert attention away from the object. All affectation of feeling that is not real, should be particularly guarded against. If there is an affectation of feeling, most commonly others see and feel that it is affectation, not reality. At any rate, the Spirit of God knows it, and will be grieved, and leave the place. On the other hand, all resistance to the Spirit will equally destroy the meeting. Not unfrequently it happens, that there are some so cold that if anyone should break out in the spirit of prayer, they would call it fanaticism, and perhaps break out in opposition.

If individuals refuse to pray when they are called on it injures a prayer meeting. There are some people, who always pretend they have no gifts. Women sometimes refuse to take their turn in prayer, and pretend they have no ability to pray. But if anyone else should say so, they would be offended. Suppose they should know that any other person had made such a remark as this, "Do not ask her to pray; she cannot pray; she has not talents enough;" would they like it? So with a man who pretends he has no gifts, let anyone else report that he has not talents enough to make a decent prayer, and see if he will like it. The pretence is not sincere; it is all a sham.

Some say they cannot pray in their families, they have no gift. But a person could not offend them more than to say they cannot pray a decent prayer before their own families. They would say, "Why, the man talks as if he thought nobody else had any gifts but himself." People are not apt to have such a low opinion of themselves. I have often seen the curse of God follow such professors. They have no excuse. God will take none. The man has got a tongue to talk to his neighbors, and he can talk to God if he has any heart for it. You will see their children unconverted, their son a curse, their daughter--tongue cannot tell. God says he will pour out his fury on the families that call not on his name. If I had time, I could mention a host of facts to show that God MARKS those individuals with his disapprobation and curse who refuse to pray when they ought. Until professors of religion will repent of this sin and take up the cross (if they choose to call praying a cross!) and do their duty, they need not expect a blessing.

Prayer meetings are often too long. They should always be dismissed while Christians have feeling, and not be spun out until all feeling is exhausted, and the Spirit is gone.

Heartless confessions. People confess their sins and do not forsake them. Every week they will make the same confession over again. A long, cold, dull, stupid confession this week, and then the next week another just like it, without forsaking any sins. Why, they have no intention to forsake their sins! It shows plainly that they do not mean to reform. All their religion consists in these confessions. Instead of getting a blessing from God by such confessions they will get only a curse.

When Christians spend all the time in praying for themselves. They should have done this in their closets. When they come to a prayer meeting, they should be prepared to offer effectual intercessions for others. If Christians pray in their closets as they ought, they will feel like praying for sinners. If they pray exclusively in their closets for themselves, they will not get the spirit of prayer. I have known men shut themselves up for days to pray for themselves, and never get any life, because their prayers are all selfish. But if they will just forget themselves, and throw their hearts abroad, and pray for others, it will wake up such a feeling, that they can pour forth their hearts. And then they can go to work for souls. I knew an individual in a revival, who shut himself up seventeen days, and prayed as if he would have God come to his terms, but it would not do, and then he went out to work, and immediately he had the Spirit of God in his soul. It is well for Christians to pray for themselves, and confess their sins, and then throw their hearts abroad, till they feel as they ought.

Prayer meetings are often defeated by *the want of appropriate remarks.* The things are not said which are calculated to lead them to pray. Perhaps the leader has not prepared himself; or perhaps he has not the requisite talents, to lead the church out in prayer, or he does not lead their minds to dwell on the appropriate topics of prayer.

When individuals who are justly obnoxious for any cause, are forward in speaking and praying. Such persons are sometimes very much set upon taking a part. They say it is their duty to get up and testify for God on all occasions. They will say, they know they are not able to edify the church, but nobody else can do their duty, and they wish to testify. Perhaps the only place they ever did testify for God was in a prayer meeting; all their lives, out of the meeting, testify against God. They had better keep still.

Where persons take a part who are so illiterate that it is impossible persons of taste should not be disgusted. Persons of intelligence cannot follow them, and their minds are unavoidably diverted. I do not mean that it is necessary a person should have a liberal education in order to lead in prayer. All persons of common education, especially if they are in the habit of praying, can lead in prayer, if they have the spirit of prayer. But there are some persons who use such absurd and illiterate expressions, as cannot but disgust every intelligent mind. They cannot help being disgusted. The feeling of disgust is an involuntary thing, and when a disgusting object is before the mind, the feeling is irresistible. Piety will not keep a person from feeling it. The only way is to take away the object. If such persons mean to do good, they had better remain silent, Some of them may feel grieved at not being called to take a part. But it is better that they should be kindly told the reason than to have the prayer meeting regularly injured, and rendered ridiculous by their performances.

A want of union in prayer. When one leads the others do not follow, but are thinking of something else. Their hearts do not unite, do not say, Amen. It is as bad as if one should make a petition and another remonstrate against it. One asks God to do a thing, and the others ask him not to do it, or to do something else.

Neglect of secret prayer. Christians who do not pray in secret, cannot unite with power in a prayer meeting, and cannot have the spirit of prayer.

The Most Important of Meetings

An poorly conducted prayer meeting often does more hurt than good. In many churches, the general manner of conducting prayer meetings is such that Christians have not the least idea of the design or the power of such meetings. It is such as tends to keep down rather than to promote pious feeling and the spirit of prayer.

A prayer meeting is an index to the state of religion in a church. If the church neglect the prayer meetings, or come and have not the spirit of prayer, you know of course that religion is low. Let me go into the prayer meeting, and I can always see the state of religion there.

Every minister ought to know that if the prayer meetings are neglected, all his labors are in vain. Unless he can get Christians to attend the prayer meetings, all he can do will not bring up the true religion.

A great responsibility rests on him who leads a prayer meeting. If the prayer meeting be not what it ought to be, if it does not elevate the state of religion, he should go seriously to work and see what is the matter, and get the spirit of prayer, and prepare himself to make such remarks as are calculated to do good and set things right. A leader has no business to lead prayer meetings, if he is not prepared, both in head and heart, to do this. I wish you, who lead the district prayer meetings of this church, to notice this point.

Prayer meetings are the most difficult meetings to sustain as they ought to be. They are so spiritual, that unless the leader be peculiarly prepared, both in heart and mind, they will dwindle. It is in vain for the leader to complain that members of the church do not attend. In nine cases out of ten, it is the leader's fault, that they do not attend. If he felt as he ought, they would find the meetings so interesting, that they would attend of course. If he is so cold, and dull, and without spirituality, as to freeze everything, no wonder people do not come to the meeting. Church officers often complain and scold because people do not come to the prayer meeting, when the truth is, they themselves are so cold that they freeze everybody to death that comes.

Prayer meetings are most important meetings for the church. It is highly important for Christians to sustain the prayer meetings, to promote union, to increase brotherly love, to cultivate Christian confidence, to promote their own growth in grace, and to cherish and advance spirituality.

Prayer meetings should be so numerous in the church, and be so arranged, as to exercise the gifts of every individual member of the church, male and female. Everyone should have the opportunity to pray, and to express the feelings of his heart, if he has any. The sectional prayer meetings of this church are designed to do this. And if they are too large for this, let them be divided, so as to bring the entire mass into the work, to exercise all gifts, and diffuse union, confidence, and brotherly love through the whole.

It is important that impenitent sinners should always attend prayer meetings. If none come of their own accord, go out and invite them. Christians ought to take great pains to induce their impenitent friends and neighbors to come to prayer meetings. They can pray better for impenitent sinners when they have them right before their eyes. I have known female prayer meetings exclude sinners from the meeting. And the reason was, they were so proud they were ashamed to pray before sinners. What a spirit! Such prayers will do no good. They insult God. You have not done enough, by any means, when you have gone to the prayer meeting yourself. You cannot pray, if you have invited no sinner to go. If all the church have neglected their duty so, and have gone to the prayer meeting, and taken no sinners along with them, no subjects of prayer, what have they come for?

The great object of all the means of grace is to aim directly at the conversion of sinners. You should pray that they may be converted there. Not pray that they may be awakened and convicted, but pray that they may be converted on the spot. No one should either pray or make any remarks, as if he expected a single sinner would go away without giving his heart to God. You should all make the impression on his mind, that NOW he must submit. And if you do this, while you are yet speaking God will hear. If Christians make it manifest that they have really set their hearts on the conversions of sinners, and are bent upon it, and pray as they ought, there would rarely be a prayer meeting held without souls being converted, and sometimes every sinner in the room. That is the very time, if ever, that sinners should be converted in answer to those prayers. I do not doubt but that you may have sinners converted in every sectional prayer meeting, if you do your duty. Take them there, take your families, your friends, or your neighbors there with that design, give them the proper instruction, if they need instruction, and pray for them as you ought, and you will save their souls. Rely upon it, if you do your duty, in a right manner, God will not keep back his blessing, and the work will be done.

Questions:

1. What was the *worst* prayer meeting you ever attended?

2. What was the *best* prayer meeting you ever attended?

3. What struck you most about Finney's teaching on prayer meetings?

Action:

Contact at least two or three friends and plan a short prayer meeting together.

afterword
Now What?

It is one thing to read a book about healthy living and it is another thing to make lifestyle changes. It is one thing to read a book about personal finance, and it is another thing to actually change your spending habits. You have now read a book about revival, but that is no guarantee that you will experience one in your lifetime.

Allow the Spirit to speak to you about the action that you need to take. Maybe look back over the areas of sin you may have seen earlier and make sure that you have done something about it. Maybe you need to find some friends to pray together for your circle of friends or church.

I leave you with a simple reminder:

> "But don't just listen to God's word. You must do what it says. Otherwise, you are only fooling yourselves." (James 1:22 NLT)

Kevin Senapatiratne
May 2014

Help in Using this Book

Pastors and leaders, your church or ministry may be closer to some exciting things that God has for it than you imagine. As you work through this book do not be surprised as God works in people's lives. My prayer is that a "season of refreshing" may come to your church or group (Acts 3:19) Here are some practical thoughts as you help lead people through the study.

This book could easily be used as an all church study over approximately a six-week period. You could read the book together at the beginning of the year or school year. The six weeks leading up to Easter would also work. If you would like to shorten it more I would recommend combining the two chapters on prayer into one week. Even if you don't normally have small groups this would be an easy way for people to meet in groups of three to ten people to discuss each chapter.

I recommend some sort of all-church prayer meetings in connection with this study. If you do not have one after every week, the weeks after "How to Promote a Revival" (Chapter 3) and after the last week would be great times to have special meetings. It is easy to have a one hour prayer meeting if you have a solid end time. In connection with this study you could even have them before or after a Sunday service.

In the small group setting encourage your leaders to allow for some time of prayer after the discussion. The leaders may not be used to leading in prayer so encourage them to read the final chapter before starting.

For the Sunday connected with each week here are some passages to get you started.

- *What a Revival of Religion Is*: 2 Chronicles 20; Acts 19:11-20, 1 Kings 18:20-39
- *When a Revival is to be Expected*: 2 Chronicles 7; Isaiah 1:18-20; Revelation 2-3
- *How to Promote a Revival*: Matthew 5-6; Romans 12:1-2; 1 Peter 1:13-16
- *Prevailing Prayer*: Luke 11:1-13; Luke 18:1-8; Hebrews 4:16
- *The Prayer of Faith*: Matthew 21:18-21; Romans 10:14-17; Matthew 17:14-20
- *Meetings for Prayer*: Acts 4:23-31; Acts 12:1-19; Acts 2

About this Book

I wanted to make a quick note about some of the technical decisions that were made in bringing Finney's Lectures on Revival to today's reader. This would be for anyone who is interested in this kind of thing.

(1) I cut down the original to a more manageable size for most readers. Not that people can't read longer books, it is just that they often don't. I figured a smaller book would also be more likely to be done in community which could provide powerful results. This means this book is only a small collection of Finney's original messages. I tried to pick ones that would lay the foundation (like the first ones) or would be a good resource for a prayer ministry like mine.

(2) In less than a handful of cases I pulled out portions of the original message. This was only if it could be done without hurting the point of the message and helped it not be as long. One example of this was to pull out a long quote when Finney is reading from Jonathan Edwards.

(3) If at all possible I kept the language "as is". That means that sometimes the wording might be a little foreign to the modern reader, but I wanted people to be able to interact with Finney as much as possible. Sometimes I updated the wording to how we use it today for ease of reading (for example changing "every one" to "everyone").

(4) I did update the scripture to the New Living Translation when possible. Again this was for ease for today's reader. If the

message however was intertwined with the wording of the passage in the original translation I left it alone.

Finney's *Lectures on Revival* is online in the public domain. If you are looking to do original research or just see the changes that I made you can compare it with one of those documents. No harm was intended with this project. The goal was simply to bring Finney's great work to another generation. Thanks!

Curtain Call

Anyone who has worked with a project like this knows that no matter the name on the cover it is a group event.

Chris MacKinnon: This project would not have become a reality without you. You really should have let me put your name on the cover with me like I asked. But then again you did the cover too!

My *Christ Connection* Board: Dwight Denyes, Vicki Higgins, Jan Jensen, Robert MacKinnon and Dan Thompson. Every ministry should be fortunate enough to have a board like you.

The *Emmanuel Christian Center* staff: Thanks for letting me hang out with all of you.

Pastor Mike Olson: For setting me on a course to long for revival.

Dr. Gordon Anderson – Your "lectures on revival" when I was in college left a mark on me.

My parents: For all your help and encouragement in life. You are helping me with my deck as I write this.

My brother, Tim: For talking me through this project.

The rest of my friends and family: I am grateful for the strength you give me.

My daughter, Samantha: I love how you love Jesus!

My wife, Jennie: "You make me want to be a better man." Love you, hon.

About Christ Connection

Christ Connection exists to ignite pastors and churches through the power of prayer ministry. Knowing the power of prayer to change churches, communities and countries we are committed to helping every Christian find a joy filled, life changing prayer walk.

Our current efforts include:

- Raising up 100,000 people to pray for pastors and leaders.
- Services, conferences, seminars and retreats on the life of prayer.
- Providing resources daily to thousands through Twitter (@EnjoyingPrayer) and Facebook (EnjoyingPrayer).
- Resourcing Pastors and Leaders through a free monthly e-newsletter "Building a Culture of Prayer".

You can learn more about our latest projects at *www.christconnection.cc*.

About Kevin Senapatiratne

Kevin is head spiritual pyromaniac for Christ Connection. He is also the author of Enjoying Prayer: Launching Your God Adventure. He founded Christ Connection in 2005 after nine years as a senior pastor in Minnesota, USA. His travels in speaking on the life of prayer take him around the United States to churches of all shapes and sizes. Having been a missionary kid for four years as a child he has a heart for the world. His ministry of prayer and preaching has taken him to four continents. He lives in Minnesota with his wife Jennie and daughter Samantha.

Spark Your Personal Revival
with new music from

EMMANUEL LIVE
and worship leader Mark Alan

Featuring 13 all new songs, including
"This is Revival (Open Up Our Eyes)"
and three special Spanish recordings

Also available
"Strong to Save"

Available on iTunes